MERSEYSIDE TRANSPORT

The 1950s–1970s

MARTIN JENKINS AND CHARLES ROBERTS

TRANSPORT SYSTEMS SERIES, VOLUME 1

Title page image: The giant floating landing stage at Pier Head was one of the seven wonders of Liverpool. *Manx Maid* (2,724grt, Cammell Laird, 1962), seen at the stage on 4 February 1963, was one of the first of the Isle of Man Steam Packet Co's side-loading car ferries and the first to be fitted with stabilisers; withdrawn 20 years later, she was eventually broken up at Garston. The other vessel is HMS *Centaur*, one of four 'Centaur'-class aircraft-carriers. Although local shipbuilders Cammell Laird launched many naval vessels this carrier was built by Harland & Wolff at Belfast in 1947, albeit not commissioned for another six years. Upgraded a decade later, she eventually carried several types of jet fighter and in 1960 was used in the film *Sink the Bismarck!*. Latterly she served as a commando-carrier and finally as an accommodation ship before being scrapped in 1973.
(Brian Faragher/Online Transport Archive)

Back cover image:The port of Liverpool benefited considerably from the development of the canal network, as merchants could now move bulk commodities to and from the Mersey more quickly and more economically. The Leeds & Liverpool Canal reached Wigan by 1777 and Leeds by 1816 and was used to transport coal and other cargoes to basins close to the city centre, while from 1848 the Stanley Cut, a flight of four locks, allowed direct access to the dock system itself. Among buildings flanking the southern extremity of the main canal were the Tate & Lyle refineries, and here one of the company's barges is seen working close to Burlington Street bridge in 1959, shortly before all commercial traffic came to an end. After Tate & Lyle pulled out of Liverpool in 1981 sections of this former industrial area were redeveloped as the Eldonian Village. (J. G. Parkinson/Online Transport Archive)

First published in 2014 as
Merseyside Transport Recalled by Ian Allen.

This edition published in 2020 by Key Books.
An imprint of Key Publishing Ltd
PO Box 100
Stamford
Lincs PE19 1XQ

www.keypublishing.com

The right of Martin Jenkins and Charles Roberts to
be identified as the authors of this book have been
asserted in accordance with the Copyright, Designs and
Patents Act 1988 Sections 77 and 78.

Copyright © Ian Allan, 2014

ISBN 978 1 913870 05 8

Typeset by SJmagic DESIGN SERVICES, India.

Introduction

Merseyside can claim, with some justification, to have provided the transport enthusiast with a greater variety of transport modes than anywhere else in Britain. By the 1950s, with many long-standing scenes about to disappear, photographers began faithfully to record what they saw in colour. It is from these collections that the authors have selected a range of images which illustrate key aspects of the richly varied scene. The book is based heavily on views from the 1950s and 1960s, although the authors have taken the liberty of including some views from the early 1970s in order to illustrate aspects which were characteristic of the core period. Using the available images, the authors have also devised a journey which takes the reader from Liverpool and its suburbs to Birkenhead and Wallasey, with one small detour to include views of the remarkable Runcorn Transporter Bridge. The journey begins with a small amount of background information.

The River Mersey and its docks

With its 31ft tidal range the Mersey is the life-blood of the area. As a result of the industrial revolution many of its tidal inlets on both banks were transformed into docks and shipbuilding yards. The first wet dock was opened in Liverpool in 1715. As trade increased and iron replaced wood and steam replaced sail, which led to ever larger ships, the dock system on the Liverpool side continued to expand until completion of Gladstone Dock in 1927. Many of these docks were built out into the river behind protective walls, and the imposing Albert Dock complex now forms part of a World Heritage Site. By the 1960s many older docks were no longer viable, and the whole south dock system closed to commercial traffic in 1972. The early history of the docks on the Cheshire side of the river is extremely complex, but the first dock opened in 1847, building continuing until the early 1930s. Bidston Dock, the last to open, is now filled in, and some of the older docks no longer handle commercial traffic. From 1858 the docks on both sides were owned and administered by the Mersey Docks & Harbour Board (MDHB). Peel Ports now operates the majority of port facilities in the area and is developing a major river berth at the mouth of the river.

Ships

Many of the world's most famous shipping lines have long associations with the port. Everything from liners to cargo boats sailed from Liverpool to all corners of the globe. Regular passenger and freight services were also operated to the Isle of Man and Ireland, and during the summer pleasure steamers offered trips to resorts along the North Wales coast. Other familiar vessels were tugs, dredgers, pilot boats, MDHB salvage and inspection ships and giant floating cranes. The last liner sailed in 1972. Containerisation and modern handling methods have reduced the number of ships in the river, but the port now handles significantly more tonnage than in the 'golden era', albeit with far fewer employees.

Ferries

There have been ferry passages across the river for hundreds of years. It was the introduction of increasingly reliable coal-fired vessels during the 19th century that led to the establishment of recognised ferry landings. Over the years these were upgraded to include floating stages and, in some cases, floating roadways to bring vehicles to and from non-passenger boats, known on the Mersey as 'luggage boats'. The ferries also encouraged population growth on the Cheshire side. At Liverpool the ferries had berths on part of the massive floating stage. A multiplicity of crossings had dwindled to just three by the outbreak of World War 2, and the New Brighton service ceased in 1971. The Mersey Ferry remains part of the scene today, albeit heavily biased towards the tourist sector.

Railways

Opened in 1830, the Liverpool & Manchester Railway was the first commercial passenger-carrying railway in the world and the first to construct a goods-only branch to serve the docks. From these exciting beginnings a network of lines was built by a variety of companies on both sides of the river. Each of these was anxious to supplement its income from passenger traffic by accessing the dock estate, with the result that many yards and goods stations were opened. On the Liverpool side MDHB locomotives eventually handled transfers between these goods depots and the quayside, whilst on the Cheshire side such work was undertaken by company-owned or private-hire locomotives. A dense local passenger network provided efficient connections within the area. The sub-river Mersey Railway (1886) was the first in the UK to convert entirely from steam to electric, in 1903, and the first to operate trains in multiple-unit formation. Likewise the Lancashire & Yorkshire Railway electrified the busy commuter line to Southport in 1904. Many local passenger stations were closed both before and after the Beeching era, as were several lines and main-line stations. Although rail access to the docks has all but disappeared today Merseyside has a network of well-used passenger services, many of which are electrified. Mention must also be made of the famous Liverpool Overhead Railway. Opened in 1893, it was the world's first electrically operated elevated railway and until its closure in 1956 carried thousands of dockers and other workers daily to their jobs.

Trams

In 1860 Birkenhead was the first place in the UK to operate horse trams. After the electric trams in Birkenhead and Wallasey were abandoned in the 1930s only the Liverpool system remained. At the end of World War 2 it was the only major system in the country still completely intact, yet despite having hundreds of new trams and miles of reserved track it was all gone by 1957. Efforts to introduce a modern light-rail network in recent years have been unsuccessful.

Buses

The first motor-bus operations in the area had begun in 1907, and these expanded rapidly. Services were provided by the municipal fleets of Liverpool (starting in 1911), Birkenhead (1919) and Wallasey (1920). These at first supplemented the trams, then gradually replaced them. The company fleets of Crosville and Ribble also developed extensive operations in the area, the latter's including a number of services worked jointly with Liverpool Corporation. The three municipal fleets – and the Mersey Ferries –- became part of the Merseyside Passenger Transport Executive (PTE) in 1969. The market changed with the advent of deregulation and privatisation in the late 1980s, notably a significant increase in cross-river bus services in competition with the trains and ferries.

Acknowledgements

The authors wish to express their gratitude to all those who have contributed photographs for this book. Particular thanks are due to the Light Rail Transit Association (London Area) for access to the Jack Wyse collection and to the Tramway Museum Society for access to the B. C. Sexton and J. J. W. Richards collections. Significant help in checking caption detail has been given by Nigel Bowker, Jonathan Cadwallader and Nigel Eames. Thanks are also due to Barry 'Curly' Cross for his unfailing support and generosity. As with the authors' other books for Ian Allan – Streets of Liverpool, Heyday of Crosville and Crosville in Colour 1965-1986 – this volume has been complied in conjunction with Online Transport Archive (OTA), a UK registered charity dedicated to the preservation and conservation of transport images and to which the authors' fees have been donated. For further information about OTA please contact the Secretary at 25 Monkmoor Road, Shrewsbury SY2 5AG (E-mail: secretary@ onlinetransportarchive.org).

Bibliography

During their research the authors drew on a number of publications, most notably Liverpool Seaport City by Neil Cossons and Martin Jenkins (Ian Allan Publishing, 2011), Liverpool Transport Volumes 3-5 by T. B. Maund and J. B. Horne (Light Rail Transit Association/Transport Publishing Co, 1987-91), British Bus Systems No 9: Liverpool's Buses by Paul Kelly (Transport Publishing Co, 1986), The History of the Birkenhead Municipal Bus Undertaking by T. B. Maund (The Omnibus Society, 2008), The Birkenhead Bus by T. B. Maund (Ian and Marilyn Boumphrey, 1994); The Wallasey Bus by T. B. Maund (Ian and Marilyn Boumphrey, 1995), Crosville on Merseyside by T. B. Maund (Transport Publishing Co, 1992), Ribble Volume 2 by T. B. Maund and A. A. Townsin (Venture Publications, 1994), Mersey Ferries Volume 1 – Woodside to Eastham by T. B. Maund (Transport Publishing Co, 1991), Mersey Ferries Volume 2 – The Wallasey Ferries by T. B. Maund and Martin Jenkins (Black Dwarf Publications, 2003), Lost Lines: Liverpool and the Mersey by Nigel Welbourn (Ian Allan Publishing, 2008), Shed Side on Merseyside by Kenn Pearce (Sutton Publishing, 1997), The Birkenhead Railway by T. B. Maund (Railway Correspondence & Travel Society, 2000), The Wirral Railway by T. B. Maund (Lightmoor Press, 2009), Merseyside Electrics by Jonathan Cadwallader and Martin Jenkins (Ian Allan Publishing, 2010) and Merseyside: The Indian Summer Volumes 1 and 2 by Cedric Greenwood (Silver Link, 2007). Much vehicle and shipping information has come from various Ian Allan and PSV Circle handbooks.

Dedication

This book is dedicated to the memory of Alan Atkinson (1948-2013) – lifelong transport enthusiast, stalwart member of the Liverpool University Public Transport Society and expert on Millom and its railways – who died just as the manuscript was being finalised.

Martin Jenkins
Walton-on-Thames

Charles Roberts
Upton, Wirral

Merseyside Transport

GEORGE'S PIER HEAD

RIGHT Our journey around Merseyside includes several visits to this once-important transport interchange. The half-mile-long floating landing stage handled everything from ferry boats to liners, whilst parallel to the stage was Riverside station, and within a short walking distance were stations on the Mersey Railway and the Liverpool Overhead Railway (LOR). During the period covered by this book Pier Head was a terminus for Liverpool Corporation buses and trams as well as for routes operated by Crosville and Ribble. In the early 1920s the area in front of the renowned waterfront buildings was redesigned to include three tramway loops (north, centre and south). In this remarkable 1926 photograph two cars are seen on the east side of the terminal. On the left of the picture is one of the balcony cars built after World War 1, while on the right, about to turn out of Water Street, is one of the city's famous Bellamy-roof trams, the last of which was withdrawn in 1949. (Claude Friese-Green, The Open Road (1926))

BELOW As the trams were phased out, loading-points for the replacing buses were scattered over the whole area. Even when an improved layout was introduced at the north end it still lacked shelters and queue barriers. Here, in September 1957, a group of women in headscarves board a well-filled 14D for one of the new postwar suburban housing estates. The suffix indicated that the bus was outbound along Dale Street as opposed to Church Street ('C'). No L146 was one of a batch of tram-replacement Leyland PD2/20s (L141-70), with 58-seat Duple bodywork, delivered in 1955. Note the coat of arms on the radiator grille and the full nearside front destination display. In the background is the steeple of the Church of Our Lady and St Nicholas ('the sailors' church'), which had been on the waterfront until George's Dock (1771-1900) was built out into the river's margins. The terminal arrangements would later be improved following the opening of a new bus station, which survived from 1965 to 1991. (C. Carter/Online Transport Archive)

LANDING STAGE

ABOVE In 1896 George's Landing Stage (ferries) and Prince's Landing Stage (liners and other vessels) were combined, the giant structure eventually measuring 2,533ft long by 80ft wide. Beneath the decking were some 200 interlinked wrought-iron pontoons which moved horizontally and vertically in order to accommodate the river's considerable tidal range. In stormy weather or during a boisterous high tide the stage seemed to have a life of its own: the bucking structure would creak and grind alarmingly, whilst the booms, mooring chains and passenger bridges securing the structure to the river wall would groan and strain against the power of the current. In July 1954 the Cunard passenger/cargo liner *Parthia* (13,362grt, Harland & Wolff, 1948) was photographed moored alongside Prince's Landing Stage. Together with her sister *Media* (1947) she covered the fortnightly Liverpool–New York service. Although slower than the larger Cunard liners both vessels carried only First-class passengers, in luxurious accommodation for 250. Proving 'rough riders', they were among the first 'Cunarders' to be fitted with stabilisers to reduce rolling in heavy seas. Each vessel had six cargo-holds, which carried anything from whisky to thoroughbred racehorses on the outward journey and mostly tobacco on the return. *Parthia* was sold in 1961 and after service with various new owners was scrapped in 1970. Also seen at the stage are two vessels belonging to the Isle of Man Steam Packet Co – the *Lady of Mann* and the *Ben-my-Chree*. (J. B. C. McCann/Online Transport Archive)

THE FLOATING ROADWAY

LEFT Access to Prince's Landing Stage was by way of a floating roadway. Enclosed within a steep cut, this 550ft-long structure designed by G. F. Lyster rested on pontoons which rose and fell with the tide, thus allowing vehicles access at all times. For many years it was used by traffic crossing the river on the 'luggage boats' operated by Birkenhead and Wallasey Corporations, which built similar roadways on the other side of the river. At low tide extra 'tip' or 'trace' horses were needed to tackle the fearsome grades. Carters also needed to exercise extreme care if the plated surface was wet and slippery. When this photograph was taken the roadway was nearing the end of its life and was being used to gain access to a temporary ferry-embarkation point whilst a new smaller ferry stage was under construction. Note the primitive 'storm' gangways in the foreground and the obelisk (left) erected in memory of marine engineers lost in the *Titanic* disaster of 1912. When the roadway closed in 1976 the area was transformed, and it now forms part of marshalling-point for vehicles using the modern ferry to the Isle of Man. (J. G. Parkinson/Online Transport Archive)

RIVERSIDE STATION AND APPROACHES

ABOVE To counteract the loss of liner traffic to Southampton the London & North Western Railway (LNWR) joined forces with the Mersey Docks & Harbour Board (MDHB) to provide direct access to the waterfront. The former replaced cable haulage with steam locomotives on its steeply graded Edge Hill–Waterloo Goods branch (1849), whilst the latter built Riverside station (opened 1895); now passengers on fast trains, including those on the four-hour 'American Specials' from London, could be conveyed directly to the landing stage. As late as 1948 there were sometimes four boat trains a day, all involving motive-power changes at Edge Hill. This photograph of Prince's Parade, taken in the direction of the Liver Building, shows the station on the left and the Customs baggage shed on the right. The overall roof dated from 1899. (A. S. Clayton/Online Transport Archive)

ABOVE The journey from Riverside to Edge Hill was filled with interest. Initially everything was at walking pace; after the train had rumbled over the Prince's Dock swing bridge a flagman walked in front of the locomotive while a policeman stopped traffic on the Dock Road, allowing the train to cross into Waterloo Goods. Once within the confines of the depot the locomotive would gather speed in order to storm the steeply graded tunnels up to Edge Hill. In 1964 English Electric Type 4 diesel-electric No D379 was photographed about to cross the swing bridge on its final approach to Riverside. Unusually, rail and shipping movements at the bridge were controlled by separate signals attached to the same mast. Most of the buildings in the background have since been demolished, although the former warehouse at East Waterloo Dock survives as an apartment block. The tugs *Kerne* and *Langbourne* belonged to the Liverpool Lighterage Co. (B.D. Pyne/Online Transport Archive)

LEFT Given its limited passenger facilities, the terminal was little more than a large transit shed. Several visits were made during organised railtours, notably one by the Stephenson Locomotive Society and Manchester Locomotive Society on 6 June 1959, when the motive power was 'Super D' No 49173. Introduced by the LNWR from 1912, these powerful 0-8-0s worked Liverpool dock traffic for half a century and, following the strengthening of the swing bridge at Prince's Half-Tide Dock in 1950, were among the heavier locomotives now assigned to the boat trains, which were sometimes double-headed. The last 'Super Ds' were withdrawn from Edge Hill motive-power depot in 1962. As some 1.7 million troops passed through the station during World War 2 it seems appropriate that the last train to leave, in February 1971, should have been a troop train. Having lain derelict for several years, the entire site was eventually cleared and is now occupied by a modern office development. (J. B. C. McCann/Online Transport Archive)

LIVERPOOL EXCHANGE

ABOVE AND BELOW Today many parts of the north end of the city are served by fast electric trains. For nearly 70 years these services departed from Liverpool Exchange station, which was located in Tithebarn Street and was close to the business and commercial districts. Replacing an older structure, it was completed by the Lancashire & Yorkshire Railway (LYR) in 1888, the trainshed consisting of four gabled roofs spanning a total of 10 platforms. At the same time the approach tracks were quadrupled to handle increasing traffic, and as early as 1904 the LYR electrified its busy Southport line. The station was severely damaged during World War 2 and was never fully repaired, so it looked increasingly dingy as passenger levels declined during the 1960s, when competing buses took people closer to the city's shopping districts and main-line services were transferred to Lime Street station. In the first view a pair of LMS-built EMUs are seen shortly before the station closed in 1977, whilst in the second No 50721, one of a class of 2-4-2 tank engines introduced by the LYR in 1889, waits to leave on an empty-stock working to the carriage sidings near Bank Hall locomotive shed on 6 August 1960. The last scheduled steam-hauled BR passenger train to arrive at Exchange, on 3 August 1968, was the 21.25 from Preston, after a spirited run behind Stanier 'Black Five' No 45318. Today only the façade survives, and in 2013 this was rebranded as the Exchange Station office development. (J. G. Parkinson/Online Transport Archive; W. Potter, courtesy Martin Jenkins/Online Transport Archive)

FIRST DOCK NORTH OF PIER HEAD

ABOVE During the construction of Prince's Dock local residents raised strong objections at the loss of the pleasant shoreline and beaches. Designed for the growing North Atlantic trade and built out into the river, the dock finally opened in 1821. At the south end there was originally a passage into George's Dock Basin, until this was in-filled to create St Nicholas Place, after which part of the passage was transformed into a small graving dock. After many changes and upgrades Prince's Dock became the base for the Irish trade. In this 1963 photograph, with the Liver Building as a backdrop, the MDHB floating crane *Birket* (777grt, Flemming & Ferguson, 1942) is transporting a mechanical digger to be loaded onto the British & Irish Steam Packet Co's *Meath* (1,590grt, Liffey Dockyard, Dublin, 1960), which was engaged mainly in the cattle trade; moored opposite is the *Ulster Monarch* (3,802grt, Harland & Wolff, Belfast, 1929), of the Belfast Steam Ship Co. The Irish trade having transferred to more modern facilities, the dock finally closed in 1981, following which it was partially in-filled to make provision for offices and hotels. *Birket* was in the MHDB fleet from 1946 to 1979. (Brian Faragher/Online Transport Archive)

THE NORTHERN DOCKS AND THE HIGH-LEVEL COAL RAILWAY

ABOVE AND BELOW The Stanley Cut enabled barges to reach Stanley Dock, one of a quintet designed for steamships by the great dock engineer, Jesse Hartley, the others being Salisbury, Collingwood, Nelson and Bramley-Moore, all five having a combined water space of 33 acres. Uniquely, Stanley was the only dock to be located on the east side of the Dock Road. In 1856 a high-level railway was built by the LYR to bring coal into the docks, and coal-drops were built at Bramley-Moore and Wellington Dock (opened 1849). Subsequent improvements to the high-level railway included additional sidings, the replacement of horses by steam locomotives and the introduction of hydraulic power, which allowed some 4,000 tons of coal a day to pass through the drops, most of this going for export or into the bunkers of steamships. Later coal for Clarence Dock Power Station was also handled here. These rare photographs, taken in May 1962, show a loaded coal wagon being moved onto the tippler located directly above the hold of a waiting ship. All movements were undertaken using hydraulically powered wires, capstans and turntables. Note that none of the men involved is wearing any form of protective clothing. The high-level railway closed in 1966, and in 2014 Bramley-Moore marks the southern extremity of the surviving commercial docks. (J. G. Parkinson/Online Transport Archive)

ABOVE An organised visit to the high-level railway in May 1962 allowed photographers to record MDHB locomotive No 30, a Hunslet 0-6-0 saddle tank of 1941, shunting in the vicinity of Nelson Dock. During World War 2 the 80-mile MDHB network handled some four million tons a year, but by 1972 this had fallen to 150,000 tons, leading to complete closure of the railway in 1973. Nowadays a section of the former MDHB main line, although much rebuilt, still provides rail access to the port. (J. G. Parkinson/Online Transport Archive)

DOCKLAND ACTIVITY

TOP LEFT Over the years the port has handled a wide range of unusual cargoes, including the world-famous LNER Pacific *Flying Scotsman* of 1923, which in 1969 was hoisted aboard the Cunard freighter *Saxonia* (5,586grt, Readhead & Sons, South Shields, 1964) by the MDHB's massive crane, *Mammoth* (Werf Gusto, Netherlands, 1920). Capable of lifting up to 200 tons, this was sold in 1986 and, now renamed, is active in Swedish waters. After a four-year sojourn in the USA *Flying Scotsman* returned home through Liverpool. In earlier times the city's first electric trams were imported through the docks from Germany and the USA, whilst in the reverse direction the city's last tram departed for the USA in 1958. (J. G. Parkinson/Online Transport Archive)

BOTTOM LEFT Although there are many colour views of ships within the docks, only a handful depict dockside activity. This bustling scene on the south side of Brocklebank Dock branch was captured in 1968 and shows the stern of the French-owned wine tanker *Noé* (2,603grt, Chantiers Dubigeon, Nantes, 1963) as well as several small mobile cranes owned by Rea's. The barrels probably contained a variety of alcohols. On the north side is one of the Elder Dempster mail boats. (J. G. Parkinson/Online Transport Archive)

CANADA DOCK

ABOVE Built specifically for the timber trade, Canada Dock (1859) was the last designed by Jesse Hartley and featured some of his trademark Gothic-style buildings; most notably, the hydraulic machinery to operate the lock gates and bridges was housed in a neo-mediaeval 'castle' (now sadly demolished). Over the years the dock underwent many changes as efforts were made to overcome silting and problems caused by the awkward angle of the river entrance. These were finally rectified in 1962 with the opening of the improved Langton River entrance, but by this time demand for traditional docks was already in decline. This view of the Harrison Line *Adminstrator* (8,714grt, William Doxford & Sons, 1958) was recorded in 1966. Today the Canada complex continues to handle scrap metal, edible oils, molasses and fish landed from Belgian trawlers. (A. S. Clayton/Online Transport Archive)

RAILWAYS AND THE WATERFRONT

ABOVE During the latter part of the 19th century the developing dock system became a magnet for railway companies anxious to benefit from the movement of bulk goods, especially timber. However, to reach the waterfront and acquire sufficient land on which to build a goods depot involved some very costly feats of engineering. For example, the five-mile LNWR Bootle branch (1866) linking Edge Hill to Canada Dock included steep grades and tunnels. Later a branch also served Alexandra Dock, and passenger services were operated to both docks until after World War 2. Overlooked by Derby Road, Hughes 'Crab' 2-6-0 No 42878 shunts within the Canada depot in 1962. This yard was severely damaged in an air-raid in May 1941, during which a large warehouse was destroyed and the Leeds & Liverpool Canal breached sufficient to flood the whole area. The yard finally closed in September 1982. (J. G. Parkinson/Online Transport Archive)

BELOW The struggle to reach the waterfront often saw the tracks of one company passing over or under those of another. The Bootle branch passed under the LYR tracks seen here, whilst the cutting in the foreground carried an LYR branch down to Bankfield goods depot. Trains departing from this yard passed through three tunnels as they belched their way through densely populated residential areas on grades as steep as 1 in 65. In April 1968 a six-car EMU formation was photographed having just left Bootle Oriel Road *en route* to Southport. It is the new Rail-blue livery introduced in the mid-1960s, the yellow stripes above the windows denoting First-class accommodation. Introduced by the LMS between 1939 and 1941 and capable of speeds in excess of 70mph, these units comprised a total of 152 vehicles and for many years were the mainstay of electrified services to Southport and Ormskirk, the last examples not being withdrawn until 1980. By the time of this photograph the two electrified tracks nearest the camera (known locally as the West Lines) were limited to peak-hour expresses and extras; until 1951 they had been used by EMUs on the service between Exchange and Aintree via Ford. As freight traffic in the area declined the West Lines were mothballed, but electric trains on the Northern Line still pass this location. (J. G. Parkinson/Online Transport Archive)

SCOTLAND ROAD AND STANLEY ROAD

ABOVE As the Overhead Railway directly served the docks, the nearest trams and buses ran a short distance inland. No colour photographs of trams appear to have been taken in this part of the city, and even bus scenes are not common. Among the busiest northern arteries were Byrom Street and Scotland Road, thoroughfares that have changed greatly since the demolition during the 1960s and '70s of hundreds of properties including houses, pubs, churches and cinemas, and the opening in 1971 of the second Mersey road tunnel led to further changes. Shortly after the formation of the Merseyside Passenger Transport Executive (PTE) No L33 heads away from the city *en route* to Kirkby. This was one of the last Liverpool buses to be delivered with an exposed radiator and was one of a batch of 60 Leyland Titan PD2/12s (L1-60) delivered during 1953 with 'Aurora'-style Weymann bodywork. More than 40 survived to pass to the PTE, among them L33, which lasted in service until 1972. In the background is The Beacon, symbol of the new Liverpool. (A. F. Gahan)

BELOW One direct route into the Borough of Bootle is by way of Stanley Road, along which Ribble 809, a Leyland Leopard with a 49-seat Weymann body, is seen heading towards the city on 22 October 1973 on service L85. Introduced in 1961, this ran from Thornton (Nag's Head) to the city terminus at Skelhorne Street. Pictured in its original livery of cherry red and ivory, 809 was one of a batch of dual-purpose vehicles delivered during 1964/5, most of which were later equipped for OMO operation, the majority being withdrawn during 1976/7. Here it is probably substituting for a double-decker. (A. F. Gahan)

BOOTLE DOCKS AND THE LIVERPOOL OVERHEAD RAILWAY

ABOVE For some 60 years the Liverpool Overhead Railway was used by those working in and around the Dock Estate, and in this 1955 scene a train is drawing into Brocklebank, one of the stations serving the northern docks. Unit 14-7-30 was one of eight three-car sets given new streamlined bodies built by the cash-strapped company between 1947 and 1955, improvements including electro-pneumatic sliding doors and upgraded lighting, seating and ventilation. Roughly a third of the seats were for First-class passengers, who travelled in much-improved accommodation. Along with restored motor car No 3, on display at the Museum of Liverpool, the short First-class, non-driving trailer No 7 from this unit also survives at the Coventry Railway Centre. Brocklebank was one of the large docks built in Bootle after its foreshore had been compulsorily purchased by the MDHB. As a result the former tranquil village was transformed into 'Brutal Bootle', much of which was destroyed during World War 2, with considerable loss of life.
(W. G. S. Hyde/Online Transport Archive)

ABOVE The Brocklebank complex included two large graving docks which could be subdivided into two smaller areas. On 2 July 1966 the Blue Funnel line cargo vessel *Melampus* (8,509grt, Vickers-Armstrong Shipbuilders Ltd, 1960) was occupying one of the subdivided spaces. This vessel became trapped in the Great Bitter Lake of the Suez Canal in the late 1960s and was not released until 1975, when she was sold to Greek owners who ran her until 1982 as the *Annoula II*. Graving docks such as these were damp and dangerous canyons, nicknamed 'pneumonia coffins' by the workers; one life-threatening job involved painting hulls with long-handled brushes from which red oxide dripped onto clothes and unprotected skin.
(A. S. Clayton/Online Transport Archive)

ABOVE When opened in the latter half of the 19th century the connected Alexandra, Hornby and Langton docks offered the most modern facilities for liners engaged in the North American trade. Designed by G. F. Lyster and constructed at a total cost of £4 million, the three docks had a combined water area of 62 acres and were able to function at all states of the tide. The walls were built of concrete-cement with sandstone facing and granite coping. On the quaysides were hydraulic cranes and a variety of warehouses and transit sheds, and electric lighting enabled vessels to dock overnight. Although Langton had been in partial use since 1873 the whole complex was opened officially in 1881. Included was this impressive block of offices for the dock master, pier master and gatemen, as well as an hydraulic engine house with a 120ft accumulator tower disguised as a clock tower. All these red-brick buildings (now demolished) were in a free Gothic style. The wooden launch *Mersey Inspector* (60grt, John Tyrell & Sons, 1963), seen here on 2 July 1966, was used by MDHB engineers and surveyors to inspect various facilities. Sold in 1972, she was later converted into a yacht. Over the years the MDHB owned many vessels, including lightships, pilot boats, salvage boats, floating cranes, dredgers and sailing flats, as well as all manner of barges. On the left of the picture is the entrance to the Langton Branch Dock, whilst behind the railway carriage (awaiting export) in Langton Street is the Alexandra Dock. (A. S. Clayton/Online Transport Archive)

GLADSTONE DOCK

ABOVE When completed in 1927 this 56-acre site featured three miles of quays, the largest graving dock in Europe, two docks flanked by transit sheds and a gated river entrance with locks. Over the years the complex was used by many memorable liners, and during World War 2 it was adapted to accommodate warships. During the years after the war the port was increasingly crippled by industrial action. When this photograph was taken on 2 July 1966 the *Empress of Canada*, (27,234grt, Fairfield Shipbuilding & Engineering, 1961) and another 'White Empress' were caught up in a damaging long-running dispute. Faced by a succession of stoppages some shipping lines opted to leave Liverpool for good. As a result of the rapid decline in transatlantic traffic the *Empress of Canada* was sold to the Carnival Line, which ran her until 1993, after which she underwent several changes of ownership before being broken up in 2003, after 42 years of service. (J. G. Parkinson/Online Transport Archive)

LEFT AND BELOW Contrasts at Gladstone. In the first picture, taken on 13 August 1955, one of a batch of locomotives built by Vulcan Foundry at Newton-le-Willows for the East African Railway & Harbours Corporation stands in the multi-gauged sidings on the west side of the dock, whilst the second shows the burnt-out hulk of the *Empress of Canada* (20,022, formerly the *Duchess of Richmond*, 1928). After catching light on 29 January 1953 the liner eventually slid onto her side. Following the most costly salvage operation in postwar Europe the stricken vessel was finally raised and sent for scrap in 1954. (J. B. C. McCann/Online Transport Archive; G. D. Parry collection)

SEAFORTH SANDS

ABOVE Seaforth Sands station was opened in 1905, when the Liverpool Overhead Railway was extended to Seaforth & Litherland over a short branch owned and electrified by the LYR. From the same date special lightweight LYR trains began operating through to Dingle, the original central power rail on the structure being replaced with the more conventional third rail, although the centre rail was retained for earthing purposes until 1921. Here, with driver Sam Robinson at the controls, set 23-11-21 loads for Dingle in 1956; car 23 was one of a batch of original Brown Marshall motor cars rebuilt in 1902/3 with full-width driver's compartments and increased seating capacity. From this station a connection led onto the LYR North Mersey branch, which for much of its length was electrified using the third rail; although the last regular electric passenger operation (Exchange to Aintree via Ford) had ceased in 1951, until March 1956 LOR trains continued to spark along the rusty third rail on Grand National days on a special Dingle–Aintree service. Seaforth Sands was the location of the company's main depot and workshops, and from 1900 to 1925 a feeder tram service operated to/from Great Crosby. (J. B. C. McCann/Online Transport Archive)

NORTH MERSEY & ALEXANDRA DOCK GOODS STATION

BELOW Built to give the LYR access to the northern docks, the North Mersey branch opened in 1866. Eventually the large North Mersey & Alexandra Dock goods station handled bulk imports such as cotton, grain and timber. A four-storey warehouse was provided, and a massive electric crane was installed for lifting baulks of timber. Shortly before closure in 1968, 'Black Five' 4-6-0 No 45284 enters the yard down the 1-in-82 grade. Overlooked by the cranes in Gladstone Dock, the diesel shunter (left) would assemble trainloads to be taken forward into the docks by MDHB locomotives and also vans and wagons filled with imports destined for massive sorting sidings at Aintree, five miles to the east. Some long-distance freights also departed directly from the yard. (Martin Jenkins/Online Transport Archive)

MDHB TRANSFERS

ABOVE On 8 July 1965 MDHB No 1, an Avonside outside-cylinder 0-6-0 saddle tank of 1904, was photographed hard at work within the dock estate, shunting a transfer train from North Mersey goods yard which consisted of various loose-coupled vans and wagons. When on the move all MDHB locomotives sounded a continuous warning bell; in addition to the driver and fireman each also carried a third man (a shunter), who, armed with his shunting pole, uncoupled wagons at pre-assigned quays and sidings. Each trainload required advanced planning, as it involved merchants and shipping lines as well as MDHB and BR officials, who had to ensure that goods were in the right place at the right time – a slow, costly procedure, with its long-established areas of demarcation, that would be swept away by the advent of containerisation. No 1 had been specially painted some months earlier for an organised tour of parts of the network by the Liverpool University Public Transport Society; in 2014 this historic locomotive remains in store. (B.D. Pyne/Online Transport Archive)

NORTH END BUS SERVICES

TOP RIGHT Catering especially for the northernmost docks, a transport hub existed on Regent Road, Seaforth. This became the starting-point for a network of tram and bus services including several peak-hour 'industrial' routes to outlying suburbs. Waiting to depart for the city on tram-replacement route 24 in 1967 is A170, a Metro-Cammell-bodied AEC Regent V. This was one of a batch of 62-seaters (A168-202) delivered during 1956/7, all of which were withdrawn by 1975. Since 1998 this area has formed part of the dock estate. (Peter Jackson)

MIDDLE RIGHT Having gained access to Liverpool in 1925 Ribble Motor Services developed a comprehensive network of local, suburban, inter-urban and express coach services, most of which passed through the northern suburbs to terminate at points within the city centre. During the period covered by this book there were four basic types of double-decker allocated to this network of Liverpool-based routes. Included were the full-front, forward-entrance Leyland PD3s delivered from 1958 with bodywork by Burlingham (1501-1605) or Metro-Cammell (1706-1800/15-50); No 1553 is pictured inbound along Crosby Road North – which until 1925 had been used by the tram service feeding into the LOR at Seaforth – on the L15 from Thornton. Although unrestored, this vehicle survives in 2014. (Peter Jackson)

BOTTOM RIGHT Liverpool Corporation operated several heavily patronised orbital routes linking the city's northern and southern suburbs. On 11 July 1974 No A288, one of a batch of 25 AEC Regent Vs (A268-92) delivered during 1957/8 with 62-seat Metro-Cammell bodies, was photographed crossing over the electrified line to Ormskirk at Orrell Park station on route 61. By now in PTE ownership, it would be withdrawn in 1976. (A. F. Gahan)

KIRKBY

ABOVE To the north of Kirkby is Simonswood Moss, where the White Moss Peat Co (which still exists) once operated an extensive 2ft-gauge system to transport harvested peat. In this view members of the Liverpool University Public Transport Society examine a Motor Rail Simplex four-wheel diesel locomotive dating from the 1940s. In the background can be seen some of the wooden-bodied peat wagons. (David Ventry)

ABOVE Kirkby underwent significant changes in 1939, when a Royal Ordnance Factory (ROF) was built on acres of agricultural land. From 1943 to 1976 there was also an internal rail network, which in wartime had a passenger station on the west side. From 1943 the ROF was also served by trams, a large turning-loop being built outside the main Administration Gate; then, early in 1944, an extension was opened to No 5 Gate/Delf Lane, where car No 766 is seen on 5 September 1954 on an enthusiasts' tour. This proved to be the last tramway extension built by Liverpool Corporation, yet such was the demand at peak times that two cars often shuttled between here and the main Admin Gate, a quarter of a mile away. No 766 was one of 12 cars (758-69) built in Edge Lane Works in 1931/2. Between 1937 and 1944 nine were modernised and re-trucked, five, including 766, surviving in service until March 1955. It was these comfortable high-speed cars, on their English Electric bogies, which had transformed the public image of the tramcar in Liverpool. (Alan Ralphs, courtesy Bolton 66 Group/Online Transport Archive)

KIRKBY TO WALTON VILLAGE

ABOVE After the war the ROF was transformed into a trading estate, and these trams are seen at the Admin Gate in April 1954, waiting for the evening exodus. In the middle of the line-up is one of the domed-roof 'Marks Bogies' (795, 818-67) named after General Manager, Walter G. Marks. The last of these 70-seaters, built at Edge Lane Works during 1935/6, survived until March 1955. During the war a private bus service had operated within the ROF, although none of the life-expired buses was licensed, as they ran entirely on private roads. (W. G. S. Hyde/Online Transport Archive)

LEFT As part of an urgent postwar drive to relocate thousands from inner-city 'slums' a new overspill town was built at Kirkby. For quite some time people relocated to the Southdene corner of the town had to trudge across windswept fields to board trams on the East Lancashire Road, where routes were reorganised but no provision was made for any shelter. Waiting to reverse on 13 March 1954 is No 812, one of the 'Cabin Cruisers' (782-94/6-817) built at Edge Lane Works in 1933/4. Designed by the City Electrical Engineer, P. J. Robinson, and influenced by contemporary cars built for London and Leeds, these handsome but heavy (18-ton) 70-seaters had a separate driver's cabin (hence the nickname), folding passenger doors and concealed interior lighting. All but one rode on EMB 'HR/2' trucks and were powered by four 27hp motors. The last three examples, including No 812, were withdrawn in March 1955. Owing to their weight and high power consumption they were latterly confined to peak-hour workings. (J. B. C. McCann/Online Transport Archive)

ABOVE AND BELOW Liverpool had one of the finest tram systems in the country, comprising some 27 miles of reserved track, including a five-mile stretch linking Kirkby with Walton Village. This featured cross-country as well as roadside and central reservations. Lengthy peak-hour loading-points were also built at Gillmoss, where two bogie 'Streamliners' are seen awaitng home-bound crowds in 1955. The 'Liners' were from a batch of 163 trams (868-992, 151-88) built by the Corporation during 1936/7. Designed by R. J. Heathman, these fast 78-seaters had four 40hp motors and a mix of different types of truck. Although their high seating capacity made them ideal crowd-shifters at peak times, three rings on the bell informed the driver the car was full up so that he could nip smartly past queues of waiting passengers, a chain preventing access to the platform. In the second view a city-bound 'Baby Grand' stands on the central reservation in the middle of the East Lancashire Road. With their high power consumption the bogie 'Streamliners' proved expensive to run, so a lighter, four-wheel version was produced, of which 100 were built at Edge Lane Works between 1937 and 1942. Despite being 3ft shorter and 25% lighter these 'Baby Grands' carried only 10% fewer passengers. Mounted on EMB flexible-axle trucks, Nos 201-300 had two 60hp motors and refurbished controllers from older cars that were fitted with EMB interlock boxes. Although not as fast as the 'Liners' they could still show a fair turn of speed. Also visible are some of the 3,500 postwar prefabs which provided accommodation for those displaced by bombing or by slum-clearance programmes. The closure of these reserved tracks coincided with the height of Suez oil crisis in November 1956, but calls for their reinstatement fell on deaf ears. In hindsight they should have formed part of a light-rail system serving the city's suburban housing estates. (Alex Hamilton/Online Transport Archive)

TOP LEFT When Gillmoss garage opened in 1962 contemporary thinking favoured large open facilities, but these soon proved impracticable. Perimeter fencing was required to prevent vandalism, bodies and paintwork suffered from exposure to the elements, and drivers and passengers complained about cold buses in the morning. This photograph, taken early in 1964, features a pair of Daimler CVs nearing the end of their working lives. They formed part of a batch of 90 tram- replacement buses delivered during 1949/50, of which 50 (D516-65) had bodywork by Northern Counties and 40 (D566-605) by Weymann, the majority also having AEC (as opposed to Daimler) engines. Note also the differing livery styles. Latterly they appeared mostly on peak-hour duties, the last examples being withdrawn in 1965. (G. W. Price)

MIDDLE LEFT Only a handful of colour images exist of trams in the city's inner suburbs. In June 1956 an American visitor captured 'Baby Grand' No 215 waiting to cross Queens Drive in order to reach the central reservation in Walton Hall Avenue. In the opposite direction cars encountered colour-light signals controlling a tightly-angled single-track section under a narrow bridge carrying the LNWR Bootle branch down to the docks. (Ray Bicknese/Online Transport Archive)

RIGHT Extra trams (and, later, buses) catered for crowds attending cricket and football matches and also race meetings at Aintree. Close to Everton FC's ground at Goodison Park additional track was also provided. Seen in April 1955, 'Baby Grand' No 263 has been driven off the main line onto a stub in Priory Road so that emergency repairs can be made to its trolley pole. This stub and the associated siding on Walton Lane were last used by football specials in October 1956. Earlier the siding was used on a couple of occasions to house displaced cars following fires at Walton depot. Liverpool's worst tram fire occurred at Green Lane depot in November 1947, when some 65 cars were destroyed. Latterly Southdene/Kirkby routes 19/44 were operated exclusively by 'Baby Grands' based at Walton. Two of these cars have been preserved. (W. G. S. Hyde/Online Transport Archive)

LOWER LANE AND CLUBMOOR

TOP RIGHT A reserved-track extension from Muirhead Avenue East to the East Lancashire Road was opened in 1943, enabling workers from Dingle and Woolton to reach the wartime establishments at Gillmoss and Kirkby. A roundabout was built at the newly created junction with the East Lancashire Road, and at peak times movements were usually controlled by a duty inspector. Here No 899 stands at the 29 boarding-point in Lower House Lane on 13 March 1954 – just weeks before the route was replaced by buses. The crew can be seen sitting in the lower saloon. This was one of 46 'Liners' sold to Glasgow during 1953/4, departing for its new home three months after the photograph was taken. A short section of this line would remain open until 5 November 1955 for use by a handful of peak-hour journeys to and from Utting Avenue East.
(J. B. C. McCann/Online Transport Archive)

MIDDLE AND BOTTOM RIGHT At several points on the system railway bridges led to breaks in the reserved track, the trams reverting to traditional street running. On 30 July 1955 city-bound No 953 passes a funeral cortege as it emerges from under the bridge carrying the Cheshire Lines Committee (CLC) North Liverpool loop line at Clubmoor. By this time the railway was closed to all passenger traffic except for Grand National 'specials', which continued until 1960. No 953 was one of 25 'Liners' refurbished in the mid-1950s, when bodywork was strengthened, seats, flooring and wiring renewed and leaks sealed (unfortunately, the 'Liners' and 'Baby Grands' suffered from water ingress). The 13/14 routes were replaced in November 1955, but No 953 survived another year, being among the last 31 'Liners' withdrawn in November 1956. After leaving Clubmoor the trams ran on the reserved track in the foreground until they encountered another railway bridge, this time on the Bootle branch, where they again reverted to street running. In the second view a train of military materials waits to cross the bridge in April 1968. (D. G. Clarke; Martin Jenkins/Online Transport Archive)

EVERTON

TOP LEFT Few colour photographs exist of buses in the older inner suburbs, but fortunately Anthony Gahan captured several superb streetscapes, among them this view recorded on 7 September 1970, just two years before Eastbourne Street disappeared altogether. Now occupied by Everton Park, this hilly area was once part of a thriving community with a rich mix of architectural styles. Owing to the narrowness of the steeply graded roads, inbound and outbound trams had run in different streets. No L233 was one of a batch of 15 Leyland PD2/20s (L230-44) which entered service in November 1956 with Crossley-framed 58-seat bodies completed at Edge Lane. Ultimately these would be amongst the last rear-entrance, half-cab double-deckers to remain in service in Liverpool with Merseyside PTE, the last example surviving until early 1977. (A. F. Gahan)

CITY CENTRE

BOTTOM LEFT Purges in the central area during the 1960s and '70s brought the wanton destruction of some very fine streets. Among these was Islington, which, after most of its stylish Georgian and Victorian buildings had been demolished, was transformed into a characterless dual carriageway. On 30 August 1972

Ribble No 1433 was captured heading for its city-centre terminus in St John's Lane (known by the Corporation as Old Haymarket). This bus was one of the last traditional rear-entrance double-deckers delivered to Ribble, during 1955/6, forming part of a batch of 120 Leyland PD2s with highbridge bodies built by Metro-Cammell (75) or Burlingham (45); among the latter group, it was one of 40 fitted with power-operated sliding doors. Vehicles of this type enjoyed a long association with Merseyside and could often be found on routes 48-59, which were worked jointly with the Corporation and numbered in its number series. (A. F. Gahan)

ABOVE In tram days the centre of Liverpool had a number of peak-hour-only loading-points, including one at Old Haymarket, which from 1950 to 1956 consisted of a three-track stub terminal. Seen on 18 June 1955, 'Baby Grand' No 264 has just arrived from Edge Lane depot and will shortly depart as an extra on route 6A. Trams ceased using this terminus on 3 November 1956, the same day they were removed from William Brown Street, Scotland Road, Byrom Street, Dale Street and Walter Street. The buildings to the left of the smoke-blackened Technical College were all subsequently demolished. (J. B. C. McCann/Online Transport Archive)

PRINCE'S LANDING STAGE, PIER HEAD

ABOVE Before turning to the eastern suburbs we pay another visit to Prince's Landing Stage. The Cunard 'Quads' launched between 1954 and 1957 were regulars at Liverpool, and here the third of the quartet, *Carinthia* (21,947grt, John Brown, 1956) is seen on 12 May 1965. Capable of speeds of 20 knots, these twin-screw liners had accommodation for 850 passengers. During the winter months they were engaged on sailings from Liverpool or Greenock to Halifax and New York, whilst in the summer they went down the St Lawrence to Montreal and Quebec. To compensate for the downturn in transatlantic passengers all four undertook more lucrative cruise work during the winter of 1966/7, but at the end of the 1967 season *Carinthia* was laid up, and the following year she was sold to the Fairland Shipping Co, which renamed her *Fairland* and, later, *Fairsea*. She was eventually scrapped in 2005 as the *Discovery*. By 1972 Liverpool had lost the last of its passenger liners, and thereafter the landing stage became ever more dilapidated. (Brian Faragher)

WEST DERBY ROAD AND MUIRHEAD AVENUE EAST

TOP RIGHT Although not as busy as the nearby Prescot Road the West Derby Road/Muirhead Avenue East corridor nevertheless enjoyed an intensive service, especially during peak hours. Seen heading into town on an all-day 18D (replacement for tram service 29) on 23 June 1969, L300 was one of a batch of 30 Leyland PD2/30s (L280-309) delivered in 1957 with Crossley body shells intended for completion at Edge Lane. However, the work was eventually done by Metro-Cammell in Birmingham, the buses finally entering service in 1961. These 64-seaters were the first Liverpool buses to have heaters, and they also had smaller destination apertures. No L300 was one of the Corporation's 18 unpainted buses. Although this attempt to reduce maintenance costs was not widely adopted, these vehicles remained unpainted until withdrawn by the PTE. Some, however, had various dashes of colour; this one sports green window surrounds. (A. F. Gahan)

BOTTOM RIGHT On 16 June 1971 Nos L137, a Duple-bodied Leyland PD2/20 of 1955, and L59, a Weymann-bodied Leyland PD2/12 of 1953, were photographed at Tuebrook on variations of route 18. In the background is the Grade I Listed Church of St John the Baptist, West Derby, while in the far distance, on the corner of Green Lane, is the Carlton cinema. Both buses are in the drab livery introduced after arrival of the first Leyland Atlanteans. By now in PTE ownership, they would be withdrawn in 1973 and 1972 respectively. (A. F. Gahan)

ABOVE At the Carlton junctions trams once diverged in three different directions, the last section to open (1923) being a tree-lined reservation along Muirhead Avenue which served one of the city's between-the-wars 'garden' suburbs. These featured well-designed houses as well as shopping arcades and libraries. After far too short a life most of this suburban light railway was abandoned on 3 April 1954. On the last day 'Baby Grand' No 270 waits to reverse at Muirhead Avenue East, having worked a 29A from the city, whilst 'Liner' 889 is inbound to Pier Head on a 29 from Lower House Lane, having just traversed the extension opened in 1943 to provide a connection with the East Lancashire Road. (J. B. C. McCann/Online Transport Archive)

RIGHT A short distance to the east of the Carlton junctions buses and trams serving West Derby crossed over the CLC North Liverpool line. Passenger traffic on this belt route declined rapidly after World War 2, West Derby station closing in 1960, and its associated goods yard in 1964. In July 1968 a freight passes through the former station. One of a batch of 36 BR Type 2s (Class 25s) built by Beyer, Peacock & Co in 1965/6, No D7630 would be withdrawn in 1981. The last section of this once busy line closed in February 1979, and today much of the trackbed is used by cyclists and walkers. (Nigel Bowker)

GREEN LANE

TOP LEFT This major link between West Derby Road and Prescot Road was used by several routes as well as by vehicles housed at Stanley Bus Park and Carnegie Road and Green Lane depots. Here an elderly AEC is seen on tram-replacement route 11 in 1965, shortly before it was withdrawn. It was one of a batch of 100 Regent IIs delivered, with minor differences, in 1946/7. Mechanically similar to the Corporation's first Regents of 1935-42, these early-postwar vehicles had more rounded 56-seat Weymann bodies but retained drop-down windows and cut-away front mudguards, which contributed to their antique appearance. Originally numbered A225-324, in 1957 they became A425-524. No A435 (A235) was one of 15 vehicles delivered in 1947, the bodies being assembled at Edge Lane. Note the former tram poles by now used for street-lighting purposes, the last trams having operated along Green Lane in April 1954. (Ron Barton)

BOTTOM LEFT Already 18 years old when photographed on 14 April 1967, No A548 was one of a batch of 100 AEC Regent IIIs placed in service during 1948/9, all with somewhat austere Weymann bodywork built to Liverpool's detailed specification and completed at Edge Lane. Originally numbered A325-424, they were later renumbered A525-624.

One of 25 fitted with preselector (rather than manual) gearboxes, A548 would be withdrawn later in 1967. The 68A was a peak-hour short working of the long-established outer-suburban orbital route 68 (Aigburth to Seaforth via Old Swan), which some 15 months later would be converted to one-man operation. (A. F. Gahan)

ABOVE One of the handful of all-day tram routes not to penetrate the central area was the 49 (Muirhead Avenue to Penny Lane via Green Lane), which was converted in September 1952. Some 17 years later the replacement 99 was one of the first bus routes to be converted to OMO. Shortly afterwards, on 4 March 1970, No 1019 was photographed heading south towards Penny Lane. Painted in a new, reversed-style livery (later dropped), it was one of 110 Leyland Panthers (1001-1110) with 47-seat Metro-Cammell bodywork (24 standees) which entered service during 1968/9. For the first time the fleet number was displayed on a small metal plate without a prefix letter indicating the vehicle make. The Panthers were among the newest of the 1,000 or so Liverpool buses passed to the PTE. However, increasing unreliability, coupled with insufficient capacity at peak times, led to the first examples being withdrawn in 1977, although 1019 would be one of the last to go, in October 1981. (A. F. Gahan)

PRESCOT ROAD CORRIDOR

ABOVE LEFT AND RIGHT In the immediate postwar era there was exceptionally heavy traffic along the Prescot Road corridor, which served old inner-city neighbourhoods, new council estates, prefabs, large factories and industrial premises. Trams ran as far as Prescot until 1949 but were then curtailed to terminate at Longview, where newly painted 'Liner' No 942 is seen in the first view on the occasion of an enthusiasts' tour in June 1952, just days before the line was further truncated at Page Moss. No 942 was one of a batch of 25 lightweight 'Liners' on Maley & Taunton trucks, all but one of which were sold to Glasgow in 1953 for £500 each. At peak times up to eight cars could be seen waiting to reverse on this crossover. In the second view No 977 is about to leave Page Moss on 5 March 1955, the last day of operation of the 10B. In addition to through tracks Page Moss had a loop, sidings and a crossover to handle peak-hour flows. Despite the number of replacement buses, trams were still needed on this busy corridor, so from 1952 to 1955 the 10B operated every 20 minutes, with additional peak-hour workings. Page Moss continued to be served by trams on route 40 until September 1957. (B. C. Sexton/National Tramway Museum; J. B. C. McCann/Online Transport Archive)

LEFT The 40 reached the city by way of a new, predominantly street-track extension. Opened in 1936, this provided a link between Knotty Ash and Oak Vale and allowed workers to reach the industrial premises along Edge Lane. Seen on the extension on 13 September 1957, 'Baby Grand' No 238 is turning from Thomas Lane onto the start of a section of reserved track along Edge Lane Drive. The next day the trams would bow out, and Liverpool would be an all-bus city, with miles of segregated reserved track left to go to seed. Trams operated on route 40 for just over 20 years. (John S. Laker)

TOP RIGHT Amongst the last buses ordered by Liverpool Corporation were the 'Jumbo' Leyland Atlanteans (1111-1235), delivery of which commenced in 1969. Long-wheelbase PDR2/1 models, they had high-capacity Alexander bodywork seating 79 or 80 passengers. No 1223 – delivered to Merseyside PTE in 1971 – is seen here when relatively new at the busy Prescot Road/Queens Drive intersection. The Old Swan area was a major interchange point where passengers transferred from the trunk east–west corridor onto peripheral outer-suburban services. In tram days peak-hour demand was such that a third track was built for 'part-way' cars, so that they would not hold up the through service. The 'Jumbos' would be withdrawn in the period 1982-4, a number operating subsequently on the Isle of Man. (A. F. Gahan)

MIDDLE RIGHT A short distance west of Old Swan is the Stanley district of the city, where Lancashire United No 289 is seen in-bound on Prescot Road just before crossing the bridge over the Bootle branch on 4 February 1971. A Northern Counties-bodied Guy Arab V, it was working one of a group of inter-urban routes linking Liverpool to such destinations as St Helens and Wigan. To the left is the entrance to Maden & McKee's scrapyard, where trams and locomotives were broken up in the 1950s and '60s, whilst behind the bus is the tower of the Corporation's Stanley Abbatoir. Behind is a Bedford TK delivery lorry from the well-known Liverpool department store T. J. Hughes. It was along this road that, from 2 July 1861, the area's first street tramway had operated, from the then boundary at Fairfield to Old Swan. (A. F. Gahan)

BOTTOM RIGHT In April 1968 Stanier 'Black Five' 4-6-0 No 44806 pauses with a short freight on the approach to Lister Drive Power Station (right), where, for some 30 years, internal movements had been handled by electrically powered steeple cabs. Following the Clean Air Act the station converted to oil power in 1963, and the bulk movement of coal came to an end. This photograph of the Bootle branch was taken from Newsham Park, which from 1955 to 1977 was home to the lower saloon of English Electric bogie car No 762 of 1931. Cut down to serve as a bowling-green pavilion, it was subsequently rescued and restored by the Merseyside Tramway Preservation Society and can now be seen on the Wirral Heritage Tramway. (Martin Jenkins/Online Transport Archive)

HUYTON AND EDGE LANE

ABOVE We cross now to Huyton and the Roby Road/ Tarbock Road roundabout, where St Helens Corporation Weymann-bodied AEC Regent V No 147 is seen on service 89F. The St Helens municipal undertaking operated a number of routes which took its vehicles beyond the town boundary, among them the 89, which provided a link with the Liverpool district of Speke (and which retains this number today as part of Arriva's network). The 89F was a peak-hour industrial service to and from Speke, the F suffix believed to stand for Ford, which company had a factory at nearby Halewood. (Peter Jackson)

LEFT One of the earliest stations on the Liverpool & Manchester Railway was named Bottom of Whiston Incline (later Huyton Quarry). Eventually it included exchange sidings for handling stone from a local quarry and coal from a number of small collieries, which arrived by means of a freight-only branch. When the station was closed by British Railways in 1958 this single-track line, known as the 'Willis' branch, remained open until closure of Cronton Colliery in March 1984. The track was lifted in 1991. Here an Edge Hill-based '8F' hauls a short coal train from Cronton Colliery towards the junction with the main line in April 1968, shortly before the end of steam. (Martin Jenkins/Online Transport Archive)

ABOVE It was Liverpool City Engineer John A. Brodie who pioneered the use of urban reserved tram tracks to serve new garden suburbs, and in 1914/5 the first of his 'grass tracks' was built to serve Broad Green and Bowring Park. For many years the privet hedges flanking the tracks were neatly trimmed, and the white fences located at crossings and stopping-points kept in a good state of repair. Originally the Bowring Park terminus was located off the main road, but as road-traffic levels increased it was relocated in 1950 to the end of the central reservation where 'Baby Grand' No 245 is seen during a farewell tour of the system on 8 September 1957. Everything in the background disappeared during construction of the M62 motorway, but No 245 was subsequently preserved and following a magnificent restoration job by the Merseyside Tramway Preservation Society now forms part of the fleet on the Wirral Heritage Tramway. (W. G. S. Hyde/Online Transport Archive)

ABOVE Sharing the Liverpool–Bowring Park corridor – and operating to Huyton and beyond – was Crosville, which company's buses were a familiar sight in Liverpool from 1925 to 1987, when its depot was closed in acrimonious circumstances. The H16 was a half-hourly service from Pier Head to Huyton Quarry and the St John's Road East estate, with a through journey time of 50 minutes. On a winter's day in the late 1960s DFG226, a 1966 Bristol Lodekka, approaches Broad Green station along Bowring Park Road. This area changed dramatically in the early 1970s with the advent of the motorway, although the houses in the background are still standing. (Peter Jackson)

ABOVE Construction of the Liverpool & Manchester Railway began in 1826. Among the many engineering achievements supervised by George Stephenson was Olive Mount Cutting, where some 480,000 cubic yards of sandstone were removed in order to create a spectacular half-mile canyon 80ft deep and 20ft wide, much of the spoil being used in the construction of an embankment at Roby and a viaduct at Sankey. When the railway opened in 1830 this cutting was regarded as a wonder of the new age. In the early 1870s the chasm was widened to accommodate four tracks. Here, in April 1968, a diesel-hauled freight bound for Edge Hill passes Olive Mount Junction signalbox as a steam-hauled goods heads towards Broad Green. The line to the right, which gave direct access to the Bootle branch, was closed in 1987. However, the chord was reinstated in 2009, and today freight trains from the docks can once again gain access to the main network without the need for a 'run round' manoeuvre at Edge Hill. (Martin Jenkins/Online Transport Archive)

EDGE LANE WORKS

ABOVE At its height this extensive works complex at Edge Hill (1928-97) employed some 1,100 people and was one of the largest purpose-built municipal transport facilities in the country. Hundreds of new trams were built here, and later scores of bus bodies were assembled and completed. Other work included rebuilding, reconditioning, repainting and overhauling both fleets. The focus of this 1963 scene is Leyland Atlantean E2, one of three experimental high-capacity double-deckers acquired by the Corporation in 1959 in order to assess their overall performance and suitability prior to placing a major order. Ultimately the Atlantean proved the most successful, and a total of 380 were delivered in the period 1962-7. No E2 had a 78-seat Metro-Cammell body with an unusual design of half-drop windows and was one of the last buses to be painted in this livery. After passing to the PTE it remained crew-operated until withdrawn in 1978 and is now preserved by the Merseyside Transport Trust. (Brian Faragher/Online Transport Archive)

BELOW Following the decision to replace the trams, withdrawn vehicles were housed on four unwired sidings laid on land between the works and the tram depot. Seen sandwiched on 'the dump' between various 'Baby Grands' in July 1957 is one of three remaining works cars which since 1943 had been the responsibility of the City Engineer & Surveyor's Department, which was also responsible for track laying and repairs. The cars were numbered in the same series as other CE&S vehicles (such as dustcarts) and were painted in the same two-tone grey. The Department even built a new rail grinder in its own workshops as late as 1948. Standing sentinel at the front of the dump is No SP1, one of four Standard trams converted into snowploughs in 1952. (E.C. Bennett and Martin Jenkins/Online Transport Archive)

THE UNIVERSITY DISTRICT

ABOVE During the past 50 years this University district has been transformed. On 8 February 1963 a pair of Leyland Titans pass building work on Brownlow Hill as they return to depot after the morning peak. No L216 of 1955 was one of 35 PD2/20s (L177-211) with Orion-style 58-seat Weymann bodies which featured a new type of full-width bonnet eliminating any bulge below the windscreen, whilst L453 was from an earlier batch of PD2/1s, of which 20 (L435-54) were delivered during 1948/9 with five-bay Leyland bodies and constant-mesh gearboxes. Most would survive until 1966/7. (G. D. Smith)

BELOW Many photographs in this area were taken by members of the Liverpool University Public Transport Society, of which both authors were members. This view features of one of the city's first 8ft-wide buses – 50 AEC Regent IIIs with 9.6-litre engines and 56-seat Crossley bodies, delivered during 1951/2. The increased width allowed for a more comprehensive front destination display. Most of these impressive buses were withdrawn *en bloc* in 1968, about half of them passing immediately to the driving school. In deplorable condition and with a trainee driver at the wheel, No A784 has just passed the University's Victoria Building (1892) and is now passing the Mechanical Engineering Department. Just out of shot to the right is the Roman Catholic Metropolitan Cathedral of Christ the King, consecrated in 1967. (G. D. Smith/Online Transport Archive)

ABOVE Further evidence of University expansion can be seen in this photograph taken on 18 June 1969 of a Lancashire United Guy Arab V passing postwar buildings in Oxford Street. It is outbound on one of the jointly operated inter-urban services to Wigan and St Helens. Dating from 1965, No 163 had a Northern Counties body and represents the large fleet of Arabs operated by LUT from the 1930s to the early 1980s. (Alan Atkinson/Online Transport Archive)

BELOW In this delightful scene, recorded in July 1957, 'Baby Grand' No 210 is turning from Crown Street into Pembroke Place as a horse drawn Corporation dust cart plods across the junction under the watchful eye of the point-duty policeman in his high-visibility coat. Two months later this same car, liberally bedecked with flags and bunting, would lead the final procession of 13 trams which passed this intersection *en route* to Bowring Park. The gaps between the properties were a legacy of the wartime bombing which destroyed so many areas of the city, most notably in May 1941. (J. A. Clarke)

LONDON ROAD/LIME STREET

TOP RIGHT To mark the closure of the tram system 'Baby Grand' No 293 of 1939 was painted in a reversed livery. Suitably adorned with 'Last Tram' inscriptions, it ran in normal service throughout the final week of operation. Another special feature was the issuing of old-fashioned Bell Punch tickets, including the long-established workmen's and children's 1d returns, which were set to disappear. The latter had allowed countless generations (including one of the authors) to ride the trams during the school holidays. With London Road as a backdrop, No 293 was photographed in Pembroke Place on the morning of 14 September 1957. In the early afternoon it worked the last 6A to Bowring Park and then in the evening took pride of place in the final procession. Today it resides at the Seashore Trolley Museum in the USA. (J. B. C. McCann/Online Transport Archive)

MIDDLE RIGHT Slightly further down London Road, at its junction with Norton Street, Ribble 1589 nears the end of its journey from Crosby on route L48 on 1 November 1969. The conductor has already set the destination blind for the return journey in order to get a slightly longer break in the canteen at Skelhorne Street bus station. This was one of 236 forward-entrance crew-operated Leyland PD3s delivered to Ribble in the period 1957-63. No 1589 was one of the earlier examples (1501-1605), being a PD3/4 model with manual gearbox and Burlingham body, and served the company from 1958 to 1974 before seeing out its days with an independent operator in the Cambridgeshire Fens. (Alan Murray-Rust/Online Transport Archive)

BOTTOM RIGHT Lime Street is probably Liverpool's most famous thoroughfare. Seen in July 1956, 'Baby Grand' No 298 has just passed the Empire Theatre (1925), where many performers have appeared, including local stars such as Cilla Black, Frankie Vaughan, Ted Ray, Ken Dodd, Arthur Askey, Tommy Handley, Jimmy Tarbuck, The Beatles and Gerry and the Pacemakers. The car has stopped adjacent to the blackened exterior of the French Renaissance-style former North Western Hotel (1871), which once attracted the rich and famous, many of whom would be sailing to the New World. After closure in 1933 it served as railway offices and since 1997 has been used as student accommodation. Beyond the tram a postman is emptying one of the many pillar boxes dotted around the central business district. (J. G. Todd/Online Transport Archive)

ABOVE In a bid to gain access to the central area the Liverpool & Manchester Railway excavated a mile-long tunnel from Edge Hill down to a new station fronting onto Lime Street. Owing to the steepness of the grade carriages were cable-hauled from 1836 to 1870. Then, to coincide with introduction of locomotive haulage, the station was rebuilt between 1867 and 1871 to include a redesigned concourse and an enlarged, curving trainshed with a crescent-shaped roof; a second trainshed was added in 1879. With the introduction of steam traction much of the tunnel was opened up to allow smoke to disperse, and between 1895 and 1900 it was widened by the LNWR to accommodate four tracks. At its height there were 11 platforms, plus a bay for banana traffic from Garston Dock. On 4 June 1966 'Britannia' No 70004 *William Shakespeare* was in charge of the second leg of the 'Fellsman' railtour organised by the Locomotive Club of Great Britain. Soon the Pacific would be tackling the sustained gradient (maximum 1 in 83) to Edge Hill, on which heavier passenger trains often required the assistance of a banking engine. Today Lime Street is the sole survivor of the city's original trio of main-line stations. (Phil Tatt/Online Transport Archive)

ABOVE For some time Skelhorne Street, on the south side of the station, was a picking-up point for a Corporation-operated express service to Speke Airport, which until the arrival of specially adapted Atlanteans was worked by four underfloor-engined Leyland Royal Tigers. As delivered in 1956 Nos SL171-4 had dual-door Crossley-bodies assembled at Edge Lane and were intended for use as one-man vehicles. However, after encountering trade-union opposition they were rebuilt by Metro-Cammell as 1½-deck coaches, the space under the raised section being used for luggage. Repainted in two shades of blue and renumbered XL171-4, they maintained the airport service until 1966. No XL173 is seen here on 18 August 1962. After introduction of the Atlanteans these 'Airporters' were redeployed during the summer to transfer passengers from the station to the Irish and Isle of Man boats. All four passed to the PTE but were sold in 1973/4, although XL171 survives in preservation. (E. J. McWatt/Online Transport Archive)

ABOVE From 1930 Skelhorne Street had been the starting-point for a number of Ribble services. Until the opening of the bus and coach station in 1960 buses were often parked unattended whilst crews took their breaks. No 2631 was one of a batch of 8ft-wide highbridge Leyland PD2/3s (2618-47/9-60) which formed part of an order originally destined for South Africa; when this was cancelled the 42 vehicles were purchased by Ribble, being delivered during 1948/9. Originally they had additional half-drop windows and destination indicators to Cape Town specification, both later being altered. Known to staff as 'Cape Towns', they spent most of their working lives on Merseyside. By 24 October 1962 the cream upper-deck band on 2631 had been painted over. Interestingly the advertisement is for the short-lived Hovercoach service between Moreton and Rhyl. The bus was withdrawn the following year. (R. L. Wilson/Online Transport Archive)

ABOVE The 1960 bus and coach station was of a two-level design built on a sloping site. The lower level, with entrance and exit for vehicles in Bolton Street, required buses to park saw-tooth-style at their designated bays and became the hub for the majority of Ribble's local route network serving Liverpool's northern suburbs and beyond. The upper floor – with access from Hilbre Street – was for longer-distance coach services and could be slightly disorganised at times, drivers having to manoeuvre carefully between passengers and their luggage. On 8 March 1971 Ribble 743, the first of a batch of 21 Leyland Leopard PSU3/3RTs with Plaxton Panorama coachwork delivered in 1963/4, waits inside the coach station. The sign directing passengers down to the bus-station concourse can be seen reflected in its windows. The whole facility closed in September 1989; following a brief second life as the Buzz nightclub the structure had been demolished by August 2002, and the site is currently in use as a car park. (Alan Murray-Rust / Online Transport Archive)

ABOVE AND BELOW Opened in 1874, Liverpool Central was the city's last main-line station and was built for the Cheshire Lines Committee, the headquarters of which were located in a three-storey office block fronting the trainshed. In 1892 the Mersey Railway was extended from James Street to terminate under ground at Central Low Level. The approach to Central had involved major engineering work which, owing to the proximity to the city centre, was undertaken without explosives. Although the station was crammed into a narrow site there were three island platforms covered by an elegant single-span roof. The first photograph shows goods and mail being assembled on the concourse and was taken before main-line services were transferred to Lime Street in 1966, following which only a local service to Gateacre remained. The second view shows the semi-derelict station shortly before closure in 1972; it was subsequently demolished. Today the twin-level subterranean station is a hub on the electrified Merseyrail network, the Northern Line to service Hunts Cross utilising much of the former CLC trackbed. The site of the High Level station has recently been redeveloped as Central Village. (Martin Jenkins/Online Transport Archive; J. G. Parkinson/Online Transport Archive (interior views))

PIER HEAD – SOUTH LOOP

ABOVE AND RIGHT The south loop at Pier Head was last used by trams on the evening of 14 September 1957, when, as the final procession set off for Bowring Park, a cacophony of ships' whistles and dockland hooters gave them a rousing send-off. Since April 1954 the remaining tram routes had all departed from the two track loop as seen in the upper view. Originally it was used by cars serving the southern suburbs. After World War 2 traffic levels were so high that an approach siding was laid in 1947, on which 'Maley' No 929 is seen on 15 May 1950 (lower view). This is the only known colour photograph of a car on route 45, which was abandoned in September 1951. (J. B. C. McCann/Online Transport Archive; C. Carter/Online Transport Archive)

BOTTOM RIGHT Having finally gained access to Pier Head in 1932, Crosville Motor Services established a network of urban, suburban and inter-urban routes, most of which served or passed through Liverpool's eastern or southern suburbs. The exposed loading-points had no protection other than rudimentary postwar shelters. Express services to such destinations as Rhyl and Llandudno sometimes required up to 20 duplicates on summer Saturdays. On 16 March 1965 various types of Bristol/ECW double-decker could be seen awaiting departure. Heading for Prescot on the H14 is Bristol KSW DKB647 of 1953; bodied (by ECW) to lowbridge configuration, with bench-style upper-deck seats and a sunken gangway on the offside, it was withdrawn in 1967. Alongside are Bristol Lodekkas DLB935 of 1958 (left) and DFB114 of 1963. Dominating the background are the Cunard (right) and Liver buildings; both have since been cleaned, while the area in front them now features a water link, enabling pleasure craft to travel between the former north and south docks. (B.D. Pyne/Online Transport Archive)

THE LIVERPOOL OVERHEAD RAILWAY AND THE SOUTH DOCKS

ABOVE Until the end of 1956 the Liverpool Overhead Railway provided a swift, reliable service for people living and working in the older southern parts of the city, close to the docks and river. Recent research has revealed that when the structure was damaged during World War 2 the LMS railway and the military authorities wanted the line to be dismantled; Liverpool Corporation indicated that it would provide replacement buses. Amazingly the LOR was also kept waiting for replacement steel. The line escaped nationalisation postwar, but by the mid-1950s it was in serious financial difficulties, and rather than meet the cost of renewing the deteriorating structure the company opted for closure. The last trains ran on 30 December 1956, Corporation buses taking over the following day. Heading this set is one of the original motor cars, which had been widened in 1902/3 to include a full-width driver's cab and extra seating; set 4-47-17 was one of just two to have 242 seats, including 38 in First class. On the left is one of the colour-light signals which replaced the original semaphores in 1921. (J. B. C. McCann/Online Transport Archive)

SOUTH CASTLE STREET, WAPPING AND CROWN STREET

BELOW A desire to introduce one-man operation prompted Liverpool Corporation to purchase significant numbers of single-deckers, including 25 rear-engined Bristol RELLs, with Gardner engines and 45-seat Park Royal bodywork, which entered service in 1969 as Nos 2001-25. The last new buses placed in traffic by the Corporation prior to its absorption by the PTE, they gave good service, the majority surviving until 1981/2. No 2002 was captured on 25 May 1972 in the lower reaches of South Castle Street.; it was along this thoroughfare that, in 1898, the city's first electric trams had travelled from their terminus located close to the Queen Victoria Monument, visible in the background. After the war many of the buildings in this area were demolished, the casualties including a maze of narrow Georgian streets, alleyways and back entries ('jiggers') close to the older docks. (A. F. Gahan)

ABOVE The southern section of the Dock Road had on its east side several railway goods stations, the oldest of which was Wapping (later Park Lane). Opened by the Liverpool & Manchester Railway in 1830, this was the first waterfront goods depot in the world and enabled the fledgling railway to increase its profits by moving goods to and from the docks. Access from Edge Hill was through the 1¼-mile Wapping Tunnel. Constructed in the period 1826-9, it was 17ft high and 22ft wide. Gas-lit from the beginning, it had whitewashed walls and a ruling gradient of 1 in 48. Until the introduction of locomotives in 1896 wagons were hauled by ropes (later cables), and, right to the end, usually descended by gravity, attached to special six-wheel brake vans. This scene shows the portal at Wapping. From here wagons were moved by wire and capstan through branch tunnels feeding into different areas of the complex. A direct link was laid into King's Dock in 1844, and in 1849 the yard was connected to the MDHB Line of Docks railway, enabling locomotives to undertake transfers between various dockside goods stations. This historic depot closed to rail traffic in 1965 and road traffic in 1972. Sadly no attempt was made to preserve the site as a 'heritage' attraction, and today it is occupied by modern industrial buildings. (J. G. Parkinson/Online Transport Archive)

BELOW When opened in 1830 Crown Street was the world's first passenger station. Until its closure to passengers in 1836 carriages were moved by cable to and from the 'Grand Area at Edge Hill', to quote a contemporary guide by James Scott Walker. Following the opening of Lime Street it survived as a goods yard and coal-supply depot and when photographed on 25 October 1968 was still relatively busy. However, the passing of the Clean Air Act led to a reduced demand for domestic coal, and the yard closed in 1972, after which the site was cleared. Also visible is one of the brick-built ventilation chimneys for Wapping Tunnel. (J. M. Ryan)

EDGE HILL

ABOVE By the 1870s the dockland goods yards were bursting at the seams, so the LNWR, which had quadrupled its share of dock traffic, invested £2 million in building a huge marshalling yard at Edge Hill with a gravity-operated gridiron which was built on a natural slope (seen in the middle of this photograph). Incoming trains of wagons were shunted to the top of the incline, from where they were despatched by gravity into the sidings so that they could be marshalled into onward trains. During the descent yard men armed with shunting poles ran alongside the moving wagons to peg down the brakes while others changed the points into the various sidings. At its height the yard had 60 miles of track and required 80 or so men to handle the daily total of up to 2,200 wagons on gradients of 1 in 50. Many older residents will recall the clink of couplings and the crashing and clanging of shunted wagons echoing around the area 24 hours a day. This overview was recorded from a somewhat precarious position on 24 November 1965. On the left, at the head of a rake of wagons, is a fireless steam locomotive belonging to Crawford's Biscuits. Following closure in 1982 the site was redeveloped as Wavertree Technology Park.
(Brian Faragher/Online Transport Archive)

TOP RIGHT After World War 2 Liverpool's six motive-power depots had a combined allocation of 320 steam locomotives, many of which were employed as dock 'trippers'. In the 1950s the largest shed, Edge Hill (latterly code 8A), had an allocation of some 120 locomotives, which ranged from powerful express types to a variety of tank engines employed to work the gridiron, shunt yards and undertake empty-stock transfers. The main site was opened by the LNWR in 1864 and over the years was progressively upgraded with improvements to the two running sheds, the coaling stage, the turntables and the ash-disposal and water-softening equipment. In 1966 a small area was rebuilt as a diesel-servicing depot, and this remained open until 1983. Afterwards the entire site was cleared and now forms part of the Technology Park. In this view a grimy 'Britannia' Pacific rests on shed on 13 June 1964, accompanied by diesels representing the new order. Part of the gridiron can be seen in the background. Many of those employed in this complex lived in the nearby streets of terraced houses. (Alan Murray-Rust/Online Transport Archive)

BOTTOM RIGHT Among classes associated with Edge Hill shed were the 'Princess Royal' Pacifics, which were regular performers on London expresses for over 20 years. Known to the Edge Hill crews as 'Lizzies', the 13 locomotives entered service between 1933 and 1935, being the first express locomotives designed by William Stanier and the first Pacifics to operate on the LMS. Here No 46207 *Princess Arthur of Connaught* storms through Wavertree on 28 May 1958, just three months before closure of the station – one of many on Merseyside to succumb before the Beeching cuts of the 1960s. (J. B. C. McCann/Online Transport Archive)

BUSES IN THE SOUTHERN SUBURBS

ABOVE As mentioned earlier, in 1959 Liverpool Corporation embarked on a vehicle-evaluation exercise to determine its future requirements. The first to be delivered was No E1, an AEC Regent V with Park Royal bodywork featuring a full front and a forward entrance with a sliding door, of very similar design to a batch then being delivered to East Kent. The Atlantean (see page 48) ultimately proved to be the winner, but E1 remained in the fleet at the end of the tests and survived long enough to pass to Merseyside PTE in 1969. It was finally withdrawn in 1974 and, after operation with a number of independents, was secured for preservation and has since been restored to its early livery style. When photographed on 8 May 1973 it was wearing the PTE's Liverpool Division livery as it operated the long, 50-minute route 81 from Bootle to Speke. This route did not penetrate the city centre but made good use of Queen's Drive, the orbital dual carriageway in the city's northern and eastern suburbs which is claimed to be Britain's first ring road. The bus is seen here on the Childwall section of the road, passing the Church of Christ the King. (A. F. Gahan)

BELOW Corporation and Crosville buses shared many streets in the southern suburbs. In this photograph, taken on 12 March 1972 at the south end of Princes Avenue, the latter's DFB23 is on service H1 (Liverpool–Warrington via Dingle, Garston and Speke), whilst the former's L738 is on the clockwise working of the Sheil Road circulars. DFB23 was one of a small batch of Lodekkas delivered in 1960 with Bristol (as opposed to Gardner) engines and was withdrawn in 1976. The Atlantean was one of a large batch (L700-879) delivered between 1965 and 1967 with slightly longer Metro-Cammell bodies, opening vents in the upper-deck front windows and two-leaf doors. The last of the L-series Atlanteans was withdrawn by the PTE early in 1982, but L738 was taken out of service some years earlier. (Anthony Drury)

RIGHT Another major artery through the southern suburbs was Smithdown Road, where A161 is seen outbound to Woolton on 16 March 1965. This was one of a batch of 67 AEC Regent Vs (A101-67) which entered service during 1955/6, all fitted with 9.6-litre engines and the Liverpool-style radiator grille, which incorporated the city's coat of arms. Nos A101-27 had all-Crossley bodies, whereas the remainder, including A161, had Crossley frames completed at Edge Lane. Virtually all of this batch passed to the PTE and were then withdrawn in the period 1970-3, following which several (although not A161) saw further use with the driving school. A short distance down the road is Hattons, the well-known transport model shop. (B.D. Pyne/Online Transport Archive)

BELOW Another of the long, straight, dual carriageways in the southern suburbs was renamed Brodie Avenue in honour of the former City Engineer following his death in 1934. At its southern end it becomes Long Lane for a short distance before reaching its junction with Woolton Road, near the location of today's Liverpool South Parkway transport interchange. On 20 May 1965 early Atlantean L679 was caught heading for Speke on route 80. A programme to convert these buses to OMO was in progress when the Liverpool fleet passed to the PTE in 1969, this particular vehicle being amongst the last to be converted, in May 1971. It was withdrawn c1976, although some of this batch survived until 1982, their appearance not improved by the removal of the unpainted skirt and repainting in the post-1974 PTE livery of Verona green and jonquil. Representing the type in preservation, L501 has been restored to its original condition by the Merseyside Transport Trust. Despite his achievements in the fields of urban planning and civil engineering Brodie is said to have been most proud of inventing football's goal net – highly appropriate for a sporting city. (Ian G. Holt)

BRUNSWICK AND HERCULANEUM

ABOVE We return now to the waterfront, where the largest and busiest of the goods facilities serving the south docks was Brunswick. For a short while passenger trains from Manchester had terminated at a station tucked in the northwest corner of the imposing CLC Brunswick goods station (background right); this arrangement ceased with the opening of the extension to Liverpool Central in 1874, but the associated yard remained and was greatly expanded. This overview shows the cranes and warehouses in Toxteth and Harrington Docks (left), Brunswick goods yard (centre) and the access tracks into Herculaneum Dock (foreground), which led to the Dingle oil terminal. Three locos are in steam, whilst a train of oil tankers (right) has just snaked out of the goods yard and is now on the main line heading south. On the extreme right is the retaining wall of the former CLC locomotive shed, closed in 1961; the yard followed in 1971, and the goods station in 1972. Today Northern Line electrics pass through this greatly diminished site, which now includes a station serving the local commercial and residential development. (Martin Jenkins/Online Transport Archive)

ABOVE Designed by Jesse Hartley and opened in 1866, Herculaneum was the most southerly of the MDHB docks. To make way for its construction a copper works and pottery were swept away. Eventually 'Herky' had coal-bunkering facilities, graving docks and an area for repairing and maintaining buoys. The first view, recorded in April 1972, shows some of the 60 casements (still extant) which are built into the rock under Grafton Street and which were used originally for storing dangerous or inflammable materials. In dock are two motor tankers, *Mabelstan* (696grt, Norrköping, Sweden, 1949) and *Peakdale H* (597grt, Groningen, Netherlands, 1968). The former (which sank off Formby Point some months later) dumped effluent at sea, whilst the latter was used as a bunkering tender. (Nigel Bowker)

BELOW Close by Herculaneum Dock was Dingle Tank Farm, where fuel was transferred by pipeline from ships anchored at jetties in the river before being moved on by road, rail or water. Access was over MDHB tracks, using fireless locomotives; these were a pair of Barclay 0-6-0s acquired in 1918, of which No 44 was destroyed during an air-raid in 1941, whilst 43 lasted until 1969 and became the last MDHB steam locomotive to be withdrawn. The latter is seen here resting within the confines of the tank farm in August 1966. (Phil Tatt/Online Transport Archive)

GARSTON AND SPEKE

ABOVE LEFT Only a handful of colour photographs of trams in the southern suburbs are known to exist, and all were taken by the late Jack Wyse in May 1951. Here No 183 speeds along Horrocks Avenue on a section of reserved track, opened in July 1939, which linked Allerton with Garston and led to a reorganisation of local services which saw the introduction of 'Garston Circle' routes 8 and 33. (W. J. Wyse/LRTA (London Area))

ABOVE RIGHT At the Garston terminus No 873 waits to depart for the city via Penny Lane. Soon it will be on the superb Mather Avenue reservation, where speeds often exceeded 45mph. This was one of the early 'Liners' on EMB heavyweight trucks and in this view is still in virtually original condition, with side indicators and wind-down windows on both decks. Later it would be among the 46 cars sold to Glasgow. Although the Corporation spent thousands of pounds on postwar track renewal the 8 and 33 were replaced in June 1953. (W. J. Wyse/LRTA (London Area))

LEFT On the same visit Jack Wyse took this rare colour photograph of a bus in the 1948 livery, with green roof and cream surrounds to the lower-saloon windows. No C625 was one of 50 tram-replacement all-Crossley vehicles (C606-55) delivered during 1948/9, all of which had DD42/7S chassis, 8.6-litre engines, synchromesh gearboxes, narrow radiators and 56-seat four-bay versions of the firm's standard five-bay body. They spent their entire working lives on routes serving the south end of the city; owing to their high fuel consumption they were latterly confined largely to peak-hour use, and all were withdrawn by the end of 1963. In the background is Garston tram depot, distinguished by its pointed roof (right) as well as the curved-roofed bus garage completed in 1940; the latter remained in use until 1996 but has since been demolished. (W. J. Wyse/LRTA (London Area))

ABOVE Owned and operated by the LNWR, the Port of Garston Docks (1853-1909) were designed to handle coal for bunkering and export. Imports included bananas, timber, metal ores and chemicals. For decades the port and its railway facilities were a source of local employment, and many terraced houses were built in close proximity. During World War 2 cargoes for Russian convoys were also assembled here. Today the docks are still open, but the remains of the once extensive rail network are mothballed, Speke Junction shed (1886) having closed in May 1968. Essentially a freight depot, it had an allocation of up to 70 locomotives, employed in local yards, on transfer work and on long-distance good trains. The last steam upgrade came in 1955, when a new mechanical coaling plant and sand-dryer were installed; in 1957 fuel tanks were provided for the growing number of diesels. Latterly the shed also became a dumping-ground for steam locomotives awaiting scrapping, some of which were less then 10 years old. After closure the vast site was cleared. Some months previously a pair of '8Fs', including No 48647, steam towards Ditton Junction, probably to work a car train from the Ford factory at Halewood. (Martin Jenkins/Online Transport Archive)

ABOVE As part of the 1920s campaign to establish municipal airports across Britain, in July 1930 Liverpool City Council opened a fine, art-deco-style airport to the designs of Edward Bloomfield on part of the Speke Hall Estate. The main buildings, including the control tower and hangars, were completed just before the outbreak of World War 2. Postwar the airport was used for some years by Dan-Air, which introduced services to Bristol and Cardiff in 1960 and for a time operated an international service to Rotterdam. In this view, recorded on 12 June 1970, veteran Douglas DC-3 Dakota G-AMPP has just landed. New to the United States Air Force in 1944, this aircraft passed to the RAF a month later and was eventually acquired by Dan-Air in 1961. Retired from use in 1970, it was initially preserved at Lasham, Hampshire, where it adopted the spurious identity of Dan-Air's first Dakota, but met an unusual fate when, having been sold to a film-production company in 2005, it was unceremoniously blown up during the making of *Die Luftbrücke*, a film about the Berlin Airlift, in which this type of aircraft played a major part. The original art-deco buildings – vacated by the airport in 1986 and replaced by more modern facilities on a new site to the southeast – were luckier, reopening as a hotel in 2001. (E. V. Richards)

RUNCORN

BELOW Between 1906 and 1961 the only way for road vehicles and pedestrians to cross Runcorn Gap was by means of the Transporter Bridge. Designed by John Webster, this was the first such bridge to be built in the UK. It was also the world's largest, with the broadest span – 1,000ft – and towers 80ft high. On 22 June 1961 thousands paid the toll to make a final crossing of the Mersey and the Manchester Ship Canal. This view shows the 'transporter' (right) and the replacement road bridge (left). (G. H. Hesketh)

ABOVE The bridge's travelling platform or 'cage' measured 55ft by 24ft 6in and was driven from a cabin located directly above it. Journey time was 2½ minutes, but in squally winds or driving rain it could be something of a white-knuckle ride. This 1950 view shows the 'cage' approaching the boarding-point on the Runcorn side. (C. Carter/Online Transport Archive)

BELOW The LNWR had spanned Runcorn Gap in 1869. Nearly a century later, in June 1962 the line from Lime Street to Crewe was electrified using the 25kV AC overhead-wire system. As a result many steam locomotives were withdrawn, including all the 'Lizzies', one of which, No 46211 *Queen Maud*, is seen waiting for the 'off' at Runcorn station in June 1959. Although the station remains in use it has, like so many on Merseyside, been modernised, and many of the original features, such as the passenger bridge and the sidings (left), have disappeared. (Derek Penney)

ST GEORGE'S LANDING STAGE

ABOVE AND RIGHT By the late 19th century the steam-powered ferry crossings which stretched from Eastham to New Brighton all had allotted berths on George's Landing Stage. The northern berths were assigned to goods or 'luggage' boats, and those to the south to the passenger ferries, most of which were operated by Birkenhead and Wallasey Corporations. The first view, dating from 1971, shows the Birkenhead gangways in their distinctive cast-iron frames. Between the two gangways is the shelter for the stagehands; until withdrawal of the night service in the mid-1950s the landing stage was manned 24 hours a day. Above it is the high-level gangway giving access to the steamer's upper or promenade deck, which tended to be used in peak hours and at times of seasonal demand. Further along is the fog bell tower (rebuilt in 1926 and now preserved at the Maritime Museum) and, to its right, part of the massive superstructure which once housed offices, waiting rooms, toilets, bookstalls and cafés. The second view shows one of the passenger bridges, which could be very steep during a low tide. Once thousands used the ferries, especially during rush hours, but following a dramatic decline during the 1960s the neglected stage was replaced in 1975 by a much smaller concrete structure, which duly sank in a gale and had to be refloated. History repeated itself in 2006 when this stage was damaged during a low tide, and a new structure opened in January 2012, the traditional hand-operated gangways being replaced by motorised units. (A. S. Clayton/Online Transport Archive; Mike Stammers/Online Transport Archive)

BIRKENHEAD WOODSIDE

ABOVE For 30 years the basic 10-minute frequency on the Birkenhead Corporation Woodside–Liverpool ferry service was provided by four almost-identical coal-fired twin-screw steamers – *Hinderton* (1925), *Thurstaston* and *Claughton* (1930) and *Bidston* (1933) – all of which were built locally by Cammell Laird & Co, which also supplied their triple-expansion eight-cylinder engines. All were 158ft 5in long, 42ft 6in, had a moulded depth of 11ft 5in. Withdrawal took effect between 1956 and 1962, the last to go being *Claughton*, seen here arriving at George's Landing Stage in 1961. A notable feature was the use of script lettering for the vessels' names. (A. S. Clayton/Online Transport Archive)

RIGHT Replacing the coal-fired steamers were three twin-screw, diesel-powered motor vessels, the first two – *Mountwood* and *Woodchurch* – being built in 1960 by Philip & Son of Dartmouth, the third, *Overchurch*, by Cammell Laird in 1962. All were licensed to carry 1,200 passengers and were powered by Crossley engines. Their dimensions were almost identical, at just over 152ft long, 40ft 6in wide and with a moulded depth of 12ft 5in. Passing to the PTE in 1969, all three have been in service for more than 50 years, although the *Overchurch* (now renamed *Royal Daffodil*) is currently laid up. Although much rebuilt and renamed after former Wallasey ferry boats these veterans provide a potent reminder of the historic significance of the Mersey ferries. In the early 1950s Wallasey Corporation took delivery of the *Leasowe* and the *Egremont*, also built by Philip & Son. (Phil Tatt/Online Transport Archive)

BOTTOM RIGHT One tradition associated with Birkenhead and Wallasey ferries was the morning constitutional. Undertaken in most weather conditions, scores of office workers (mostly men) paraded in an anti-clockwise direction around the upper deck. This view recorded in the late 1950s on a Birkenhead steamer highlights the smart but somewhat drab array of hats and mackintoshes. Overall capacity on these classic vessels was 1,433. (A. Southern, courtesy G.D. Parry)

ABOVE Following withdrawal of the luggage-boat service in 1941 the floating roadway at Woodside was retained to bring coal onto the stage for the passenger steamers until 1955, after which the passenger bridges were used. Latterly the north end of the floating stage was used as a tug berth. In 1968 this mixed bunch of tugs owned by J. H. Lamey Ltd and the Rea Towing Co Ltd was probably waiting for the tide to enable them to assist vessels in and out of the Birkenhead docks. Included are motor tugs *William Lamey* (1959), *J. H. Lamey* (1964), *John Lamey* (1927) and *Edith Lamey* (1942), the latter two having been converted from steam tugs. Also present is oil-fired steam tug *Applegarth* (1951), along with two of her sister vessels. Behind the stage are some of the once extensive cattle lairages, where animals were taken for sale, slaughter or trans-shipment after being off-loaded at the Wallasey stage, a little way to the north. Many had arrived 'on the hoof' from Ireland, a practice which continued long after the introduction of refrigeration. When the wind blew in a certain direction the pungent smell from these lairages carried as far as New Brighton. Towering over the scene is the ventilator shaft for the Queensway road tunnel, which opened in 1934. This tunnel led directly to the demise of the luggage-boat service, with the result that the *Oxton* and *Bebington* were requisitioned for vital war work in 1941. Fitted with derricks and assisted by a Wallasey luggage boat, they

off-loaded more than 11,000 US-built aircraft. The stage was replaced by a much smaller structure in the 1980s. (Geoff Davies/Online Transport Archive)

OPPOSITE TOP This imposing station (1878-1967) which occupied the south side of the Ferry Approach was opened when the LNWR and Great Western (GWR) Joint line was extended from Green Lane Junction. Designed by R. E. Johnson, its iron-arched trainsheds spanned seven tracks with five wide but short platforms, which restricted to eight the number of carriages on longer-distance trains. It was actually designed the wrong way around: the intended front entrance was never used as such and ended up as a parcels office, with the result that a side entrance was used. In its heyday more than 80 staff were employed, trains departing for destinations as far afield as Bournemouth, London, Margate and the North Wales coast. In March 1967 Stanier 2-6-4T station pilot No 42616 was photographed waiting to assist the London (Paddington) train (left) up through the curving tunnel with its 1-in-95 gradient *en route* to Rock Ferry. Although regarded by many as being worthy of preservation the building was demolished after closure on 4 November 1967. Latterly much of the glass was missing from the roof façades, and the concrete lamp standards [seen here] had replaced earlier, more ornate gas lamps. (A. S. Clayton/Online Transport Archive)

BELOW Woodside was the starting-point for many Birkenhead Corporation bus routes, some of which replaced the trams between 1925 and 1937. Birkenhead operated mostly Leylands until World War 2, and after the war 45 PD1s (101-45) with 56-seat prewar-style Massey bodies were delivered during the period 1946-8. When No 123 was photographed in September 1957 it was in the 1950 version of the undertaking's livery, with cream surrounds to the lower-deck windows, sans-serif lettering and the word 'Corporation' omitted from the fleetname. These were the first buses to have heaters and sliding (as opposed to half-drop) windows. When new they also had rear bumpers, which were removed in 1954. The final examples were withdrawn in May 1963, but No 105 has been restored and can nowadays be found at the Wirral Transport Museum in Birkenhead. (C. Carter/Online Transport Archive)

TOP LEFT Impressed by the rugged, reliable Gardner 5LW engines in 36 utility Guys delivered in the years 1943-6, Birkenhead placed further orders for Guy Arabs. Those delivered during 1949/50 (146-60/91-205) were fitted with the larger (8.4-litre) 6LW engine. All had the traditional timber-framed 56-seat Massey body, with curved end windows to the lower saloon, with the exception of No 201, which had the prototype Massey metal-framed body with square lower deck windows. This 1964 view of 197 shows the new, lower bonnet line. The last of this batch were withdrawn in 1966, some examples joining the driver-training fleet. (E. C. Bennett/Online Transport Archive)

MIDDLE LEFT No 227 was one of a batch of 15 Guy Arab IIIs (226-40) delivered in 1952 with 8ft-wide 59-seat East Lancs bodies. All were withdrawn during 1968, although five joined the driver-training fleet, the last two surviving until 1971. On the far left of this 19 September 1966 picture is the off-peak parking area, which accommodated three lines of tightly-packed buses. With the closure of the station and the decline in cross-river ferry traffic Woodside gradually reduced in importance as a transport hub. However, the ferry still operates – albeit on a much-reduced frequency – and a few buses call at a small, redesigned bus station, while on certain days a heritage tram service starts in front of the ferry building (1864). (Alan Murray-Rust/Online Transport Archive)

BOTTOM LEFT The Corporation's small fleet of single-deckers was allocated to New Ferry depot for use on route 44, which passed under a low railway bridge. From 1948 to 1964 this route was home to four Leyland Tiger PS1s (97-100) with 33-seat, rear-entrance Massey bodies. Upon delivery it was discovered that 97 had been issued with the duplicate registration ACM 106, and it was hastily issued with a new number. In this view it is very much 'off-route' and is possibly on its way to or from Laird Street for maintenance. In the background are the station, Town Hall spire and Woodside Hotel, finally demolished in 2008. (G. Parry)

TOP RIGHT After protracted and often acrimonious negotiations Crosville gained access to Woodside in 1930, although restrictions were placed on picking up and setting down within Birkenhead. A complex network of local, suburban, inter-urban and express services was rapidly established, with many duplicates provided during the season, especially to popular destinations in North Wales. On 14 September 1957 two vehicles were photographed on variations of route 1, which served the lucrative Birkenhead–Chester corridor. To the fore is ML742, an early (1955) Bristol Lodekka, complete with 'long apron' radiator grille and 60-seat ECW body, whilst behind is MW648, a Bristol KSW with 55-seat ECW body, new in 1953. Both had Bristol engines and each has its original front destination display; both would be withdrawn in 1970. Note the conductress in her headscarf, as well as the sign pointing along Rose Brae, which spanned the station throat and led to the parcels area on the south side. This bridge was removed in 1958 when local ship repairers Grayson, Rollo & Clover extended their premises to the perimeter of the station. (C. Carter/ Online Transport Archive)

MIDDLE RIGHT This view recorded on 25 August 1967 features the north wall of the station and SLG201, a 1951 Bristol LL5G with a 39-seat rear-entrance ECW body, working service F7 to Mill Park Estate. When withdrawn the following year this was one of the last Crosville half-cab single deckers to operate on the Wirral. The ferry approach was built between 1858 and 1866 on reclaimed land. (Peter Jackson)

BELOW RIGHT For many years the neighbouring borough of Wallasey also favoured Leylands. Pictured on 19 May 1952, No 15, one of a batch of PD1s (11-34) delivered in 1948, passes the Mersey Motor Co works in Bridge Street as it departs for New Ferry on route 10, the busiest of the jointly operated cross-docks services which carried heavy traffic between and within each borough. Over the years variations were made to its routeing, especially in the vicinity of Hamilton Square, and although it did not directly serve Woodside ferry terminal it passed within walking distance. Sometimes long queues formed for 10s heading into Wallasey, and on occasions frustrated residents opted to walk home across the docks. This view was recorded shortly before advertisements appeared on Wallasey buses. The 1948 PD1s were the last buses to be delivered with offside indicators and drop-down windows, whilst the small holder on the offside of the driver's cab was used to display cards publicising local events. (C. Carter/Online Transport Archive)

BIRKENHEAD TOWN CENTRE

ABOVE Hamilton Square owes its origins to William Laird, founder of the Birkenhead Iron Works (later Cammell Laird & Co Ltd). He envisaged an elegant grid of wide streets radiating from the square, on which work began in 1826. In the event his vision evaporated rapidly following the opening of the docks and the construction of rows of terraced houses. Pictured navigating the square on 4 December 1966, No 260 was one of a batch of 10 Leyland PD2/12 (256-65) delivered in 1954 with 59-seat 'Aurora'-style Weymann bodywork, all of which were withdrawn between 1969 and 1973, this particular example spending some time in the driving-school fleet. Stretching into the distance is Cleveland Street, used by trams until 1935; this was also the main route to Duke Street Bridge, the principal crossing-point over the docks into Wallasey. (Alan Murray-Rust/Online Transport Archive)

BELOW Situated at the end of Mollington Street, relatively close to the town's business, commercial and entertainment district, was Birkenhead loco shed (shed code 6C; 8H from 1963). A joint LNWR/GWR facility (1878), with sheds for both companies, it had replaced earlier structures and was built on the filled-in Tranmere Pool. Over the years the area was steadily upgraded, the last major improvements to the steam facilities being completed in 1955. On Sunday mornings in the mid-1960s as many as 70 locomotives could be seen simmering 'on shed'. Nearest the camera in this view is grimy '8F' 2-8-0 No 48535, and alongside is No 42727, one of the last serviceable Hughes 'Crab' 2-6-0s; these locomotives had a long association with Birkenhead, the last survivor being withdrawn after working a passenger duty from Woodside on 31 December 1966. Towards the end of steam local enthusiasts were often allowed to clean locomotives and, in the case of No 42727, to repaint the smokebox numberplate and shed plate. After losing its final allocation of 47 steam locomotives in November 1967 Mollington Street remained as a diesel depot until November 1985. The large site was subsequently cleared but remains largely derelict. (Martin Jenkins/Online Transport Archive)

SINGLETON AVENUE AND PRENTON

RIGHT Birkenhead's association with Guy Motors dated back to 1926, when it took delivery of three short-lived single-deckers; then came the 36 wartime 'Utilities' described earlier. In 1953, in order to prolong their lives, the Corporation overhauled 15 chassis and had them fitted with new Gardner 6LW engines and metal-framed Massey bodies built to an unusual width of 7ft 9in. These rebodied vehicles re-entered traffic as 241-55, of which the last is seen climbing Singleton Avenue during the evening peak on 6 November 1969, just days just days before withdrawal. No 242 was acquired for preservation and now resides at the Wirral Transport Museum. (Alan Murray-Rust/Online Transport Archive)

BELOW In October 1965 routes 79 and 80 were combined to form the Prenton Circle, on which No 355 is seen passing the photographer's car in Prenton Hall Road on 29 March 1972. This was one of a batch of seven Guy Arab IVs with Gardner 6LW engines delivered during 1955 with 59-seat Massey bodies similar to those fitted to the rebodied Guys described above. The following year an additional 15 Arab IVs entered service with a mix of Massey (10) and East Lancs (5) bodies, and these proved to be the last of this make. They had no cream waistbands, and the fleetname 'Birkenhead Transport' was displayed on the lower panels on either side of the coat of arms. Having passed to Merseyside PTE in 1969, all would be withdrawn by 1972. (Alan Murray-Rust/Online Transport Archive)

NEW FERRY–HOOTON

ABOVE Following its opening in 1840 the Chester & Birkenhead Railway grew rapidly into a heavily used line with a link into the docks. From 1844 to 1878 the Birkenhead terminus was at Monk's Ferry, where passengers could take a ferry to Liverpool. The ferry service was withdrawn when Woodside opened, but the branch stayed open for freight (mostly coal) until 1961. The first station at Rock Ferry (1862) was replaced by a new, six-platform building in 1891. At the same time the Mersey Railway gained access to Rock Ferry, although the company had to pay the LNWR & GWR Joint for running rights as well as for use of two terminal platforms; four goods lifts were also installed to handle the volume of parcels traffic between the Mersey Railway and the main line. After Woodside closed in 1967 trains from the south terminated at Rock Ferry, this arrangement continuing until the third rail was extended in stages to Chester and Ellesmere Port between 1986 and 1993. This April 1966 photograph shows Stanier 2-6-4T No 42613 drawing into the station with a semi-fast to Chester. (Martin Jenkins/Online Transport Archive)

BELOW This view of New Chester Road was recorded in 1964 and shows 360 on the South Circle route 85. Dating from 1955, this was one of seven Guy Arab IVs (355-61) with 59-seat Massey bodies and Gardner 6LW engines, all of which were transferred to the PTE; sister vehicle 359 was the last Guy to operate in Birkenhead. Some of the buildings on the right have since been demolished, among them the Corporation bus garage, which closed in 1973. Until 1931 trams on the New Ferry route had terminated in this area. (G. D. Parry)

BROMBOROUGH

RIGHT Among the first industrial premises to be built along the waterfront between Tranmere and Eastham was a factory opened in 1855 by Price's Patent Candle Co of London on the banks of Bromborough Pool, with berths for ships and a garden village for the workforce. When William Hesketh Lever established his industrial empire on the banks of the tidal inlet in 1888 he also built, for his workers, a model settlement which he named Port Sunlight after his popular product, Sunlight Soap. Located between the river and Port Sunlight, Bromborough Port was developed on Lever-owned land. In this view the Blue Funnel Line *Autolycus* (7,420grt, Vickers-Armstrong, 1949) is in dock with her funnel painted in the colours of the Nigerian National Shipping line, to which she had been on charter. She was docked in Bromborough for lay-up after service on the West African liner trade. It was often alleged – though officially denied – that the heavily polluted waters of Bromborough Dock killed off accumulated marine growth on a ship's hull; it is more likely that berthing charges for ships laid-up here were competitively low. The other vessels seen here are grab-hopper dredger *Cressington* (1,431grt, A. & J. Inglis, 1962), bucket dredger *Beaver Chief* (629grt, Scheepswerf & Machinefabriek De Klop, Netherlands, 1957) and motor-hopper barge *Barrow Deep* (911grt, A. Hall & Co, 1926). Bromborough Dock was closed at the end of 1986 and filled in, although a narrow channel was left for the River Dibbin to make its way through the site and thence into the Mersey. Mersey Wharf still handles bulk imports and exports. (Nigel Bowker)

ABOVE *Duchess of Kent*, an Andrew Barclay 0-4-0 diesel of 1955, stands outside the Stork Margarine works on 26 October 1963. Lever Bros had its own 52-mile railway system which included connections to Bromborough Dock and the main line. Many of the wagons and brake vans, often acquired from BR, were restricted to internal use. From the 1960s the railway handled less and less traffic, the final rail movements taking place in the vicinity of the Soap Works in June 1984. However, a short section was reconstituted as a BR works line for the conveyance of hot edible oil from 1988 to 1992. At its height the Lever system had an internal passenger service, and the dock and port became heavily congested during World War 2, when it was used as an adjunct to Liverpool. (E. V. Richards)

ABOVE When the Chester & Birkenhead Railway opened in 1840 it was single-track throughout, but passing-places were soon installed, notably at Hooton, one of the first stations on the new line. The volume of goods traffic steadily increased, and the line was quadrupled as far Hooton in the early years of the 20th century, stations being rebuilt and bridges widened to accommodate the new lines. This increased capacity proved vital during both world wars. Pictured on 4 June 1965, ex-LMS Hughes 'Crab' 2-6-0 No 42783 hauls a long mixed goods onto the 'old' main-line tracks north of Hooton station. Following the quadrupling these had become the up and down fast lines; the 'new' slow lines and Hooton North signalbox can be seen to the left. Alongside the row of railway cottages on the right is an animal-feed factory. Hooton had become a junction in the 1860s, when lines to Helsby and Parkgate (later West Kirby) were opened. The former provided a more direct route towards Manchester and remains open today, but all traffic on the latter ceased in 1962. Reduction of the four tracks began in 1967, although some sections survived for a time as sidings. Nowadays the remaining double-track line is electrified between Rock Ferry, Ellesmere Port and Chester on the third-rail system. (E. V. Richards)

HOOTON–WEST KIRBY LINE

TOP AND MIDDLE RIGHT Neston, on the west side of the Wirral Peninsula, once had two stations – one on the Great Central line and one on the LNWR & GWR Joint branch from Hooton. In the first view, recorded on 7 August 1954, ex-GWR '51xx' 2-6-2T No 4129 pauses at Neston South (formerly Neston) station en route to Hooton. The station had once handled coal traffic from a nearby pit, closed in 1927. For much of its length the line hugged the east bank of the River Dee, most of its stations being some distance from centres of population. Once competing buses began operating into Birkenhead people deserted the trains, but in the line's heyday Heswall had boasted its own peak hour First-class club carriage. Increasing losses led to the closure of two stations in 1954 and the withdrawal of the full passenger service on 15 September 1956, when 'Large Prairie' tank engine No 4122 worked the last train from West Kirby. Adding to the sense of occasion were a couple of vans transporting circus elephants, which, alarmed by exploding detonators, were trumpeting loudly as the train left the station. Until final closure on 7 May 1962 the line was used for goods and excursion traffic, driver-training on DMUs, troop movements to an RAF base at West Kirby, van traffic to a Cadbury's factory at Moreton and for taking Wirral-based EMUs for overhaul at Horwich. In the second view a 'Jinty' 0-6-0 works bunker-first on a goods train through Hadlow Road station on 12 August 1961. This station is now preserved, and much of the right of way forms part of the Wirral Way, opened in 1973. (J. B. C. McCann/ Online Transport Archive; J. M. Ryan)

BOTTOM RIGHT In 1896 the basic network of railways serving the Wirral was completed with the opening of the line between Hawarden and Bidston. This quickly became part of a Great Central (GC) service from Wrexham to Seacombe, where passengers bound for Liverpool could either take the Wallasey ferry or connect with the Mersey Railway at Birkenhead Park by changing at Bidston. The isolated station at Burton Point did not open until 1899; however, being some distance from any centre of population, it was closed on 5 December 1955. Much of the site was still intact 11 years later, when a Derby-built DMU was photographed passing *en route* to New Brighton. Today the station building and platforms remain (albeit heavily overgrown), but the footbridge and platform-level waiting rooms have been demolished. (Phil Tatt/Online Transport Archive)

BEYOND THE BIRKENHEAD BOUNDARY

TOP LEFT In return for granting Crosville access to Woodside, under the terms of the 1930 agreement with that company Birkenhead Corporation was granted powers to operate to places beyond its boundaries, such as Eastham, Bromborough, Frankby, Heswall and Thurstaston. In 1972 No 370 was photographed on route 96, which crossed the entire Wirral Peninsula from Woodside to Thurstaston in a journey time of 44 minutes. By now most journeys were curtailed at Greasby, where the picture was taken. No 370 was one of 25 Leyland PD2/12 delivered in 1954/5, with bodywork by three different manufacturers, 367-71, received in 1955, having 59-seat Weymann 'Orion' bodies. These five vehicles were withdrawn in 1972/3. Note the period roundabout sign and the view towards Saughall Massie, Moreton and Liverpool Bay in the background. (Geoff Davies/Online Transport Archive)

BOTTOM LEFT Impressed by the Gardner engines fitted to its wartime Guys, Birkenhead ordered two batches of Daimler CVG6s (161-90) with Gardner 6LW engines for delivery in 1949/50, all with 56-seat Massey bodies. In this view, recorded on 13 August 1961, No 187 heads along Thingwall Road, Irby, on the Summer Sundays-only route 74 to Thurstaston Shore. In the event of inclement weather two of the three scheduled journeys were suspended. The Daimlers would be withdrawn between 1963 and 1966. (J. M. Ryan)

UPTON AND BIDSTON

ABOVE In the dying days of BR steam increasing numbers of photographers came to record the iron-ore workings between Bidston Dock and the John Summers & Sons steelworks at Shotton. To handle this traffic new marshalling yards were laid at both ends, and the former GC line underwent major strengthening to accommodate 1,000-ton trains; these were hauled originally by ex-LNER locomotives from Bidston shed, but in 1955 the latter received an allocation of '9Fs'. Developing a tractive effort of 40,000lb, these 2-10-0s were ideally suited for the steep climb from Bidston to Neston, and following closure in 1963 of Bidston shed more than 50 were eventually allocated to Mollington Street. Pictured on 2 July 1967, No 92045, one of the first to arrive on the Wirral, slogs up Storeton Bank, where the gradient was 1 in 75. A '9F' could haul up to eleven 88-ton hoppers plus a 20-ton brake van, the load sometimes exceeding 1,150 tons, but despite this the only brakes were on the locomotive and the guard's van. On a crisp, clear night the exhaust from these toiling firebrands could be heard echoing across the north end of the peninsula. At first the ore trains operated around the clock, but complaints from residents led to the night workings being stopped, and some people even managed to secure a reduction in their rates. (E. V. Richards)

ABOVE Many of the stations in the area covered by this book originally had a goods yard and, in some cases, additional bays and sidings for handling agricultural produce and livestock. For more than a century coal delivery was a lucrative business for the railways and local merchants, but many yards closed in the 1960s as the demand for coal declined. In this busy scene '8F' No 48436 shunts the yard at Upton on 31 October 1967. Earlier in the day the same locomotive had worked a morning iron-ore run to Shotwick (eight hoppers only) and a van train from Cadbury's factory at Moreton. Upton yard closed in 1968, and the site is now occupied by a Co-op supermarket. Replacing these yards, a coal-concentration depot existed at Birkenhead North from 1964 until 1993. (Martin Jenkins/Online Transport Archive)

LEFT Locomotives assigned to the iron-ore trains were allocated initially to the former Great Central shed (1897) at Bidston, where existing facilities were improved. Initially Class O4 2-8-0s were used, as was the occasional '8F', but following the arrival of the first '9Fs' in 1955 these 2-10-0s gradually took over most of the work. Two of the original allocation – Nos 92046 and 92047 – are seen on shed at Bidston, which closed on 11 February 1963, not long after this picture was taken. Known to the crews as 'Spaceships', the '9Fs' were transferred to Mollington Street, along with a few 'Jinties' and 'Dock Tank' No 47164. (G. Parry Collection/Colour Rail 313948)

BOTTOM LEFT Among the handful of known colour photographs of the ex-Wirral Railway Seacombe branch (1895) is this one taken from Seacombe Junction signalbox in 1959. In the foreground BR Standard Class 3 tank No 82021 is working a three-coach train to Wrexham. While on the right a '9F' stands in the iron-ore sidings at Bidston Dock, waiting to begin the 13-mile journey to the steelworks. Having acquired running rights over the branch, the GC introduced its Seacombe–Wrexham service in 1898, although restrictions were in force with regard to picking up and setting down on the Wirral Railway network. Never especially busy, there were 12 passenger workings a day when the branch closed on 3 January 1960. Goods traffic continued as far Oakdale sidings until December, after which a short section was retained for wagon storage until 1963. Part of the M53 motorway and Kingsway Tunnel approach road now follow much of the course of the branch. (E. C. Bennett/Online Transport Archive)

ABOVE The Mersey Railway was the first in the UK to convert entirely from steam to electric. The American-style wooden-bodied motor cars and trailers, built by G. F. Milnes in 1903, had clerestory roofs and matchboard panels. The bogies and electrical equipment were imported from the USA, the motor cars having four 100hp motors and air brakes; later, master controllers were added to the driving trailers, allowing multiple-unit operation. Subsequent deliveries, including replacements for war-damaged stock, had more modern, domed ends, wider windows and elliptical roofs. Following electrification of the LMS lines to New Brighton and West Kirby in 1938 the Mersey Railway stock was adapted to run on the third-rail system and was also fitted with a 'dead man' facility; in later years the age of these units gave rise to the nickname 'Grandad's Railway'

in the local press. The final examples were withdrawn in June 1957, and this photograph, taken shortly afterwards at Birkenhead North, shows the last of the old trains waiting to go for scrap. They had offered an exhilarating ride, with much arcing, especially on frosty evenings, when massive flashes would illuminate the night sky. (J. B. C. McCann/Online Transport Archive)

BELOW With their lightweight all-steel saloon bodies the LMS's new EMUs for the 1938 electrification offered a high degree of comfort, and in 1956 virtually identical units replaced the old Mersey Railway stock. Powered by four 135hp motors, the last of these long-serving units (BR Class 503) were withdrawn in 1985, although one set has been preserved. This view overlooking Bidston Moss was recorded in 1959. (E. C. Bennett/Online Transport Archive)

BIRKENHEAD DOCKS – SOUTH SIDE

ABOVE Although the MDHB owned virtually all the tracks serving Birkenhead's docks, warehouses and yards it operated no locomotives, so shunting movements were handled, under strict regulation, by locomotives belonging to various contractors or to the major railway companies (later BR). Among the latter were some of the 10 powerful 'Dock Tanks' designed for the LMS by Henry Fowler. Dating from 1928, these versatile 0-6-0s had short, fixed wheelbases for negotiating tight curves. No 47164 is seen near Poulton Bridge Road in the late 1950s. Although BR officially dispensed with the use of steam shunters at Birkenhead Docks in 1961, one 'Dock Tank' continued to work within the Vacuum Oil Co's premises on the south side of the West Float until 1963. Early in 1956 this locomotive had gone to the Cromford & High Peak Railway to assess its suitability for use on the steeply graded line. (John Collingwood/Online Transport Archive)

BELOW For years all manner of discarded buses were scattered around the Dock Estate. This early-1965 view features Birkenhead 341 [(left)], one of the utility Guys, still in virtually original condition. Dating from 1944, it was one of four with angular Park Royal bodies which originally had wooden-slatted seats, although 341 was later fitted with moquette seats and given the rear destination boxes from a 1936 Leyland Titan TD4. All four were withdrawn in 1954. As the 'Utilities' were prone to over-heating they often ran with the bonnet hood partially open; when working cross-docks routes 10 and 11 they tended to boil over, especially when waiting for Duke Street Bridge to be lowered or for a slow-moving train to rumble across, and as a result watering cans were strategically positioned in the Duke Street area. On the right of the picture is 188, a 1950 Daimler with 56-seat Massey body, its Gardner 6LW engine having been removed. (E. J. McWatt/Online Transport Archive)

PARK STATION/CLAUGHTON

ABOVE A short distance from Duke Street is Birkenhead Park station, which until 1938 was the interchange-point between the electric Mersey Railway trains and the steam-hauled LMS services to New Brighton and West Kirby. Since 1924 it had also been a terminus for Crosville routes serving the more affluent parts of the Wirral Peninsula. The loading-point in Beckwith Street had a waiting room and an inspector's hut. Buses departed by way of Cavendish Street, and on 25 September 1970 No DLB935 was recorded turning into Park Road North, outbound to Fulton Avenue, Newton. This 1958 Bristol-engined Lodekka had an 60-seat ECW body and was withdrawn in 1971. Crosville would cease using Birkenhead Park station in 1979, when its route network was integrated with that of the PTE and its buses began running through to Woodside. (Anthony Drury)

BELOW Among the Corporation routes using Park Road North were those to and from Moreton. Inbound towards Woodside on 21 March 1970 was No 157, one of a batch of 13 Leyland Atlanteans (155-67) delivered in 1968 with 77-seat Northern Counties bodies. Originally crew-operated, they were all eventually converted for OMO. Among 224 buses which passed from Birkenhead Corporation to the PTE, they were withdrawn in the early 1980s. When delivered in 1969 Birkenhead's last Atlanteans (168-82) had front entrances and centre exits. (Alan Murray-Rust/Online Transport Archive)

ABOVE The most numerous postwar type in the Birkenhead fleet was the Leyland PD2, some 180 examples entering the fleet in the period 1951-67. This evocative view of Tollemache Road was recorded on 7 March 1970 and features Massey-bodied No 10, which had entered service early in 1958. Most of the PD2s survived long enough to pass to the PTE, some examples surviving until early 1977. This vehicle passed into the training fleet and subsequently into preservation with a local group. (Alan Murray-Rust/Online Transport Archive)

BELOW The last Guys to enter service were 15 Arab IVs with Gardner 6LW engines, delivered in 1956. The 59-seat bodies, which had flashing direction indicators from new, were built by Massey (372-81) or East Lancs (382-6). Here 386, the highest-numbered bus in the fleet, passes through Claughton on the cross-town 51A from Port Sunlight to Upton on 29 March 1972. Most of these vehicles were withdrawn shortly after passing to the PTE.
(Alan Murray-Rust/Online Transport Archive)

BIRKENHEAD DOCKS

TOP RIGHT The first docks to open were Egerton and Morpeth, in 1847. After early problems the docks on both sides of the river became one estate, with control and management vested in the MDHB as of 1 January 1858. With Liverpool handling some 45% of the nation's exports, further docks on the Birkenhead side were urgently needed, with the result that the Wallasey Pool was transformed by 1860 into the Great Float dock system. However, reliable access was achieved only when Alfred Dock and its associated river-entrance locks and vestibule dock were opened, in 1866. Further improvements came in 1928 with the opening of new entrance locks and a second passage from Alfred Dock into the East Float. Early in 1973 Blue Funnel's *Elpenor* (7,757grt, Harland & Wolff, 1954) was photographed manoeuvring in Alfred Dock. Renamed *United Concord* in 1978, it would be broken up the following year.
(Geoff Davies/Online Transport Archive)

MIDDLE AND BOTTOM RIGHT When these photographs were taken the Great Float had five miles of quays and 112 acres of water. Some moorings within were often used by vessels awaiting disposal or for winter lay-ups. The Liverpool & North Wales Steamship Co's *St Tudno* (2,326grt, Fairfield Shipbuilding & Engineering Co, 1926) and the Isle of Man Steam Packet Co's *Lady of Mann* (3,104grt, Vickers Armstrong, 1930) were both firm Merseyside favourites. Here the former (bottom) is seen awaiting scrap in the East Float at Vittoria Wharf Cross Quay, having made her last voyage on 16 September 1962, while the latter (top), which only operated during the summer months, is seen in the West Float at Cavendish Wharf, having been prepared for her final season in 1971 before being withdrawn that August. Identifiable by her distinctive cruiser stern, 'The Lady' was the largest steamer owned by the IoM Steam Packet Co. In the background of the second picture are some of the flourmills established on both sides of the Great Float, while on the left is the floating crane *Mammoth*, with its 200ft jib and twin smoke stacks, which was sunk here in May 1941; deemed vital to the war effort, it was raised reportedly on direct orders from Winston Churchill. (A. S. Clayton/Online Transport Archive (both))

ABOVE On the day Morpeth Dock opened a trainload of guano was taken from the quayside onto the Chester & Birkenhead Railway. Eventually company-owned goods stations were established within the dock estate, the MDHB having been obliged to provide free rail access to the docks and quays. The large GWR station on the north side of Morpeth Dock gave the company access to markets in Liverpool, most of its cargo crossing the river by barge until 1922 and in part on the Wallasey luggage-boat service until 1947. In the late 1920s the station was enlarged and modernised with sidings for some 850 wagons. Fast, vacuum-fitted good trains were advertised with apposite names such as the 'Meat', the 'Feeder', the 'Birmingham Market', the 'Cambrian Pioneer', the 'Farmer's Boy', the 'Flying Skipper' and the 'Northern Docker'. Seen in the spring of 1967, No 73135, a BR Standard Class 5 4-6-0 with Caprotti valve gear, has just left Morpeth and is rumbling over Egerton Bascule Bridge (now preserved); the two Dock Board employees armed with red flags are stopping any road traffic. The yard closed just over five years later, by which time it was the last BR goods station in the docks. The severed tracks on the right served various premises on Shore Road, including the lairages at Woodside, which in the mid-1950s were still sending some 200 cattle wagons daily by rail. (Martin Jenkins/Online Transport Archive)

TOP RIGHT In the first of two photographs taken on 3 August 1958 a mixed goods hauled by 'Crab' 2-6-0 No 42854 crosses 'D' bridge, between Egerton Dock (right) and the West Float, on its way to The Sough (pronounced 'suff'), a four-track freight cutting passing through central Birkenhead, in order to reach the main line at Green Lane. In the background is 'C' bridge, another of the four bridges giving access to Wallasey. These lifting bridges, all of which carried railway tracks, were erected in the early 1930s to replace first-generation swing bridges, which themselves had replaced an earlier embankment in 1867. (J. B. C. McCann/Online Transport Archive)

BOTTOM RIGHT The second view shows the complex layout controlled from Canning Street North signalbox. The track leading to the Four Bridges can be seen on the left, together with various goods depots, including the LNWR Egerton Dock goods station of 1873, part of which survives today. The small building in the centre of the picture was the joint GWR/LNWR traffic office. Seen on the right, No 11119 (later D2503), a Hudswell Clarke 0-6-0 of 1956, was one of the first BR diesel shunters assigned to the docks; here it has descended The Sough and is en route to the MDHB main line, which started a few yards beyond the signalbox and over which rail movements ended in 1993. The former BR section of line is now disused, although much of the track remains, while the former Dock Board section may be converted for light-rail use as part of the Wirral Waters redevelopment. (J. B. C. McCann/Online Transport Archive)

SEACOMBE AND THE DOCKS

LEFT For many years Seacombe was an important bus/ferry interchange. The introduction of steam-powered ferry boats had transformed Wallasey into a significant dormitory town for Liverpool, with more than 40% of the adult population at one time crossing the river to work in the city. In 1926 a new three-berth floating stage was installed, along with a floating roadway. The luggage-boat service ceased in 1947, and the honour of being the last steam ferry on the river fell to the *Wallasey*, which was built by the Caledon Shipbuilding & Engineering Co of Dundee in 1927. Measuring 151ft 4in in length, 48ft 1in across the beam and with a moulded depth of 14ft 5in, she had a passenger capacity of 2,233; converted to oil-burning shortly after the end of the war, she was reconditioned by Harland & Wolff in 1958. Reflecting a downturn in passenger numbers, the long-standing two-boat, 10-minute service had only recently been reduced to a 20-minute, one-boat off-peak service when this photograph was taken on 9 May 1963. After making her final crossings later in the year the *Wallasey* went for scrap in February 1964. The stage seen here was replaced in 1999. (B. D. Pyne/Online Transport Archive)

BELOW Although relations between the Corporation's bus and ferry committees were often strained, the public expected co-ordinated connections, and in 1933 an impressive new terminal was opened. Arriving buses offloaded outside the ferry building, with its imposing clock tower, before moving forward to reverse (under the watchful eye of the conductor), herring-bone-fashion, into assigned loading bays on the south side, passengers waiting under a covered colonnade. During rush hours the duty inspector would blow his whistle, whereupon up to 15 fully laden buses, including several 'part-ways', would depart simultaneously for all corners of the town, the whole process being repeated 10 minutes later. The arrival in 1958/9 of the first Leyland Atlanteans broke this pattern, although a couple of rear-loaders can be seen here still adhering to the herring-bone tradition in September 1967. The buses on the left were parked between peaks. In 1969 around 70 Wallasey buses passed to the PTE, although several were already out of service. (Marcus Eavis/Online Transport Archive)

ABOVE Corn warehouses were first established on the south side of the East Float in 1868, the grain originally being despatched to inland mills. From the 1890s major firms such as Joseph Rank's and Spiller's built their own mills on the waterfront, so that by the 1930s the combined total made Merseyside the second-largest flour-milling centre in the world. Today there are no working flourmills, although some of the buildings have been transformed into apartments. Here the Swiss-owned *Basilea* (6,211grt, Flensburger-Schiffbau Gesellschaft, 1952) is seen after unloading her cargo in 1967. (Geoff Davies/Online Transport Archive)

BELOW The first section of the rail system laid by the MDHB on the north side of the Great Float was opened in 1873. Eventually various goods stations were established, most shunting being carried out by private contractors. After World War 2 BR had also hired out diesel shunters at competitive rates. However, as tonnage gradually withered away the former company goods stations were closed. In the period 1969-72 the Wirral Railway Circle organised several dockland tours, the third of which, the 'Birkenhead Docker III', was run on 1 July 1972 in conjunction with the Liverpool Locomotive Preservation Group. A rake of brake vans and open wagons was double-headed by Lucy and Efficient, both of which had been housed in William J. Lee's small loco shed on Birkenhead Road, Seacombe; the former was an Avonside 0-6-0 saddle tank of 1909, the latter an Andrew Barclay 0-4-0 of 1918. Today both are at the Ribble Steam Railway in Preston. This photo stop on the Dock Road was alongside one of the massive quayside mills, some of which were badly damaged during the war. (Geoff Davies/Online Transport Archive)

ABOVE Duke Street Bridge, which divides the East and West floats, also marked the boundary between Birkenhead and Wallasey. In 1873 railway tracks were laid across the original toll bridge of 1861, which was replaced by the present bascule bridge in 1931. This 1968 photograph shows one of Birkenhead's ubiquitous Leyland PD2s emerging from the north side *en route* to New Brighton on the jointly operated route 11. As the movement of ships had priority over road traffic, Wallasey residents would allow 90 minutes to make this unpredictable cross-docks journey in order to catch coaches and trains at Woodside. (Geoff Davies/Online Transport Archive)

BIDSTON DOCK

TOP RIGHT Located at the western extremity of the Great Float, Bidston Dock (1933) was enlarged to handle imported iron ore for onward transhipment to Bidston Steel Works and, later, John Summers Iron & Steel works at Shotton. In the first view, recorded on 3 October 1964, three massive unloading cranes tower above the fully laden *Knightsgarth* (10,780grt, Blyth Drydock & Shipbuilding Co, 1961), owned by William Cory & Son Ltd. Once offloaded, the ore was shunted from the quayside to the BR exchange sidings by diesel locomotives owned by Rea Ltd. (H. B. Christiansen/Online Transport Archive)

BOTTOM RIGHT The second view, recorded shortly before the end of steam, shows part of the exchange sidings where the ore trains were assembled. To mark the end of steam haulage '9F' 2-10-0 No 92203 made a valedictory run on 6 November 1967; the replacement Class 47 diesel locomotives (an example of which is seen on the right) sometimes had problems hauling the heavy loose-coupled ore trains. Following rationalisation in the steel industry this traffic ended in 1980, after which the cranes were occasionally used to discharge other bulk cargoes until dismantled in 1992. The dock was filled in between 2001 and 2003. (Martin Jenkins/Online Transport Archive)

MORETON

ABOVE Having started life as a shanty town, the parish of Moreton was incorporated into Wallasey in 1928, after which the latter introduced new bus routes to compete with those operated by Birkenhead Corporation since 1919 and Crosville since 1920. The subsequent battle for traffic was intense, both Corporations offering competitively priced combined bus/ferry tickets. This photograph at Moreton Cross was taken on 13 June 1968, shortly after the introduction of some single-deck, one-man-operated Crosville routes linking Birkenhead and Wallasey with Hoylake and West Kirby. ERG52 was one of a batch of 10 dual-purpose Bristol RELLs (ERG52-61) with 50-seat ECW bodies delivered in 1968. Withdrawn in 1981, it was subsequently preserved by a Wirral-based group. (R. L. Wilson/Online Transport Archive)

TOP RIGHT Birkenhead Corporation buses first reached Moreton Shore in 1927. On fine days the sand dunes and the funfair attracted thousands, who also arrived by train and, later, by bus from Wallasey. Shortly after delivery a new Daimler Fleetline waits to return to Woodside on 9 September 1964. This was one of a batch of nine vehicles (101-9) with 77-seat front-entrance Weymann bodies and Gardner 6LX 10.45-litre engines. They wore this simplified livery from new, reportedly to speed up delivery from the factory, but were repainted in standard livery after a couple of years. These were the last Daimlers bought by the Corporation, and after passing to the PTE they were withdrawn in 1977/8. At this time the bus was crew-operated. The conductor, in his grey jacket, is standing by a classic Birkenhead bus stop, its red 'BCT' finial indicating that this was a fare stage. (E. J. McWatt/Online Transport Archive)

BOTTOM RIGHT For a few short weeks during the summer of 1962 people watched the comings and goings of the world's first commercial passenger-carrying hovercraft service, which began operating between Moreton Shore and Rhyl on 20 July. Operated by British United Airways Ltd, the Vickers VA3 hovercraft had four turbine engines, a top speed of 60 knots and seating for 24. The fare for the 15-mile, 20-minute journey was £1. As the service survived only until 14 September 1962, colour views are quite rare. (Phil Tatt/Online Transport Archive)

WALLASEY

ABOVE Wallasey's main shopping centre was located at Liscard, which was served by a number of bus routes including the jointly operated cross-docks service 9, which ran through to Charing Cross. Seen waiting to depart in the late 1960s is Birkenhead Corporation 268 of 1954, one of five Leyland PD2s (266-70) with 59-seat Ashcroft bodywork, the styling of which was clearly influenced by contemporary Massey and East Lancs designs. The lower and upper decks were built in the newly opened Ashcroft premises in Birkenhead Dock Road, but, owing to the low height of the building, the two halves had to be joined together at Birkenhead's Laird Street depot. These were the only bus bodies built by this local firm, funding coming from Vernon's Pools as part of a philanthropic drive to provide local employment. All five Ashcrofts survived to pass to the PTE but would be withdrawn by 1973. (Online Transport Archive (photographer unknown))

BELOW Among Merseyside bus garages demolished during the past 30 years was the former Wallasey depot at Seaview Road. Opened in 1902 to house the new fleet of electric trams, the substantial site also included a power station, an office block and a row of houses for senior staff. Additional garage space and a new workshop were provided in the late 1920s. This photograph was taken inside the original running shed, shortly after the formation of the PTE. On the left is ex-Wallasey Leyland Atlantean No 12 (by now Merseyside PTE 212); the other two Atlanteans are 194, a Northern Counties-bodied vehicle which had been ordered by Birkenhead but not delivered until after the formation of the PTE, and 1292, an Alexander-bodied example dating from 1972. No 194 displays the number for one of the newly introduced cross-river routes which offered a fast link between Wallasey and Liverpool by way of the Kingsway Tunnel. All three buses are in the Wirral Division livery of dark blue and pale lemon, representing the colours of the constituent Birkenhead and Wallasey fleets. Seaview Road depot was a casualty of deregulation in October 1986 (all operations being concentrated thereafter at Laird Street, Birkenhead), and the site is now occupied by an Asda supermarket. (E. J. McWatt/Online Transport Archive)

ABOVE As part of the celebrations marking Wallasey's 50 years as a borough a parade of four buses was held on 18 June 1960. To represent the 36 all-Leyland Titan TD1s delivered to the Corporation in the late 1920s this preserved Bolton Corporation TD1 was painted in Wallasey's original bus livery of primrose green and cream. This photograph shows the cavalcade pausing outside the Cemetery Gates in Rake Lane; the other vehicles were a horse bus (from Manchester), a PD1 (seen here) and an Atlantean. In line with its prewar policy of replacing vehicles after eight years, Wallasey had sold its last TD1s in 1939. (A. S. Clayton/Online Transport Archive)

NEW BRIGHTON

BELOW Founded in the early 1830s as an upmarket dormitory for Liverpool, New Brighton rapidly became a magnet for holidaymakers and day-trippers, and on fine days thousands would arrive by bus, coach, ferry and train. The former Wirral Railway station (still extant) has an island platform with a long concrete canopy, added at the time of electrification in 1938, together with off-peak and overnight storage tracks on both sides. The goods and coal yard seen here on the left were closed in 1965, the site now being occupied by industrial buildings. Following closure of the Seacome branch in 1960 the replacing DMUs on the Wrexham service were initially re-routed here. On certain Bank Holidays, some of these workings reverted to loco haulage and were described in the supplement to the working timetable as 'made steam and retimed'. This practice continued until 1966, two sets of non-corridor coaches being retained for the purpose. Photographed on Whit Monday (7 June) 1965, pannier tank No 4683 of Croes Newydd shed runs round its train before taking on water. (Martin Jenkins/Online Transport Archive)

ABOVE LEFT AND RIGHT The station was close to several bus routes, one of which, the 15 (formerly 5) terminated adjacent to the Winter Gardens theatre-cum-cinema (1931), which ended up as a Bingo Hall before being demolished and the site redeveloped for sheltered housing. In the first of two photographs taken on 14 September 1957 the conductor of No 104 changes the destination blind to show Seacombe Ferry. The body was one of six completed by Burlingham in 1949 and fitted to six prewar Leyland TD4c chassis, which then took the numbers 102-7. Subsequently, in 1955/6, the bodies were transferred to six new Leyland PD2/10s, all of which would be withdrawn during 1965 as a result of service reductions and route closures. In the second view No 90, one of the first batch of 24 postwar Leyland PD1s (78-101) delivered in 1946 with 56-seat Metro Cammell bodies, is seen on tram-replacement service 17, which followed a circuitous route to Seacombe and would be discontinued in 1967. The last of this batch of PD1s was withdrawn in 1960. (C. Carter/Online Transport Archive)

TOP RIGHT Most routes serving New Brighton arrived and departed via Rowson Street, which in tram days was the scene of several runaways. Pictured in 1968, No 64 climbs the steeply graded hill on tram-replacement route 14. Seen in the livery introduced in 1961, this was one of a batch of Leyland PD2/12s (59-80) with 56-seat Weymann bodywork, delivered during 1951/2, which were the first 8ft-wide vehicles in the fleet and the first to feature two-track route-number blinds. Most passed to the PTE, the last examples not being withdrawn until 1974. Many properties in the area at one time offered 'B&B' accommodation. (Online Transport Archive/Photographer unknown)

BOTTOM RIGHT Wallasey was the first municipality to operate the new and as yet unproven rear-engined Leyland Atlantean, the first entering service on 8 December 1958. Ultimately the Corporation would acquire 30, the last being delivered in 1961. All had 77-seat front-entrance bodywork by Metro-Cammell. On the first day Atlantean No 1 (now preserved) was assigned to route 1 with a crew of four – a driver (who struggled with the new type of gear control), two conductors (one upstairs and one down) and an inspector (who alighted at each stop to direct bemused passengers to the front of the vehicle). It had been hoped that the Atlanteans would enable the Corporation to dispose of older vehicles retained for peak-hour use only. Sometimes, in off-peak periods, they were operated as one-man vehicles with the upper deck closed off until one-man operation of these large double-deckers was authorised in 1966. This photograph of No 10, still in traditional livery, was taken in Virginia Road shortly after delivery. The loading-stands, which stretched along much of this road, were invaluable for marshalling large holiday crowds. Sometimes demand was so heavy that buses were double-parked with their engines running. (Phil Tatt/Online Transport Archive)

ABOVE LEFT Among New Brighton's many attractions was an 18in-gauge miniature railway, opened in 1947. Most of the equipment, including the locomotive *Tim Bobbin* and three enclosed coaches, was acquired by local showman and entrepreneur Tommy Mann from a closed line near Clacton in Essex. Officially named the Fairy Glen Miniature Railway, the ¼-mile line ran from a station adjacent to the Promenade, the trains following a tightly packed circuit which featured a tunnel with a miniature fairground. Such was its popularity that a second, conventional coal-burning 4-4-2, *Crompton*, was acquired in 1951. In the mid-1950s this was given a streamlined body recalling the 'Coronation' Pacifics of the LMS and is seen here in 1958 with one of the saloon coaches of 1936. As late as 1959 an ex-War Department diesel locomotive was added to the fleet. When New Brighton's fortunes went into steep decline in the 1960s there was a 95% drop in the numbers employed in the hotel, catering and entertainment industry. Tommy Mann's railway was one of the casualties, closing in 1965, its rolling stock being dispersed to other lines and collectors. Today New Brighton is enjoying something of a revival. (Phil Tatt/Online Transport Archive)

ABOVE RIGHT Arguably the most memorable Mersey ferry boat was the diesel-electric *Royal Iris* (1,234grt, Denny & Bros, Dumbarton, 1950) which entered service in April 1951 in a striking livery of cream and green, her dummy funnel housing a fresh-water tank. Designed to carry 2,296 passengers when on ferry service and 1,000 on cruise work, she had four Ruston & Hornsby diesel engines, a streamlined superstructure incorporating a main deck, shelter deck and sun deck, a dance floor, an ice-cream and cocktail bar, a

tea bar and a fish-and-chip restaurant. Initially dubbed 'the floating fish-and-chip shop' and derided by more conservative residents, she slowly endeared herself to generations of Merseysiders. She was ideal for working lucrative cruises, which provided the cash-strapped Ferries Department with much-needed revenue and also proved useful during times of peak demand on the New Brighton service, being seen here heading back to Liverpool in the late 1960s. Faced with a decaying stage, silting problems and a severe drop in passenger numbers, the New Brighton ferry closed in September 1971; the pier had been demolished by 1974, and the neighbouring promenade pier by 1977. The *Royal Iris* was eventually sold in 1993 and at the time of writing (2014) is moored in a derelict state on the River Thames. (E. J. McWatt/Online Transport Archive)

BELOW LEFT Our tour of Merseyside ends where it began, at the world's largest floating landing stage. Recalling the glory days, a packed three-decker embarks for New Brighton in 1958. Built locally by Cammell Laird & Co, she was launched in 1934 as the *Royal Daffodil II*, the prefix having been granted by King George V in recognition of the heroic role played by the original *Daffodil* and *Iris* of 1906 at Zeebrugge during World War 1. This memorable name is now carried by one of the present ferry fleet. Initially she was licensed to carry nearly 2,000 passengers, but after 1955 the figures were 1,982 when on ferry service and 850 when cruising. During World War 2, on 8 May 1941, she was hit by a bomb and sank at Seacombe stage, fortunately without casualties (although the chief engineer did lose his dentures). After being raised in June 1942 she was reconditioned by local firm Grayson, Rollo & Clover and re-entered service a year later. Converted to oil in 1947, she was renamed *St Hilary* in 1957 (anticipating the arrival of another *Royal Daffodil II* in 1958) and was finally sold for scrap early in 1962. Since this photograph was taken the stage has gone, and the waterfront buildings have been cleaned. A limited ferry service still runs, but mainly as a tourist attraction. (G. W. Morant/Online Transport Archive)